Painting World War II Miniatures

Mike Davidson

Text written with and photography by Jeffrey B. Snyder

I0809168

Schiffer Publishing Ltd

4880 Lower Valley Road, Atglen, PA 19310 USA

To Kim Jones, whose imagination, wit, talent, and friendship have made this hobby so much fun for over twenty-five years.

Copyright © 1997 by Mike Davidson
Library of Congress Catalog Card Number: 97-80075

All rights reserved. No part of this work may be reproduced or used in any form or by any means—graphic, electronic, or mechanical, including photocopying or information storage and retrieval systems—without written permission from the copyright holder.

This book is meant only for personal home use and recreation. It is not intended for commercial applications or manufacturing purposes.

Book Design by: Laurie A. Smucker

ISBN: 0-7643-0371-6
Printed in China

Acknowledgments

I would like to thank Owen Reynolds for his photographic work on the front cover.

I would also like to thank Chris Mrosko of Warrior's Scale Models and Dave Bighia of Yanks Miniatures for their help on this book. Warrior Scale Models and Yanks Miniatures are available at fine hobby shops or by contacting Warriors Scale Models, Inc., 519 S. Raymond, Pasadena, CA 91105, and Yanks Miniatures, 3731 Schuemann Drive, Omaha, NE 68123.

Published by Schiffer Publishing Ltd.
4880 Lower Valley Road
Atglen, PA 19310
Phone: (610) 593-1777; Fax: (610) 593-2002
E-mail: schifferbk@aol.com
Please write for a free catalog.
This book may be purchased from the publisher.
Please include $3.95 for shipping.
Try your bookstore first.

We are interested in hearing from authors
with book ideas on related subjects.

Introduction

Military miniatures depict all historical periods from ancient times to the modern armies of today. Perhaps the most popular are those that show the uniforms and equipment of World War II soldiers.

The painter has a huge variety of World War II figures from which to choose, ranging in approximate height from 54mm to 200mm. From the deserts of North Africa to the frozen steppes of Russia and the hot, humid jungles of the Pacific to the mountainous terrain of Scandinavia, almost every theater of operation and type of uniform is depicted in one size figure or another.

The focus of this book is to introduce the hobbyist to the basic techniques and color combinations that can be used when painting World War II figures. The uniform color mixes provided are by no means the only colors that can be used, but are a good starting point when painting figures of this era. I encourage the figure painter to experiment with different combinations of colors.

The figures used in this book are produced by Yanks Miniatures and Warriors Scale Models, Inc. They are typical of the high quality of today's commercially produced World War II miniatures.

I hope this book will be useful when painting figures from this very interesting period of military history.

Contents

Military Miniature Clubs

Historical Miniature Society of Northeastern Oklahoma
5526 S. Toledo Place
Tulsa, OK 74135

Military Miniature Society of Illinois
P.O. Box 394
Skokie, IL 60077

Southern California Area Historical Miniature Society
220 Tola Pl.
Anaheim, CA 92804

The Atlanta Soldier Society
P.O. Box 669843
Marietta, GA 30066

Historical Miniature Figure Society of Colorado
4805 Pitkin Way
Aurora, CO 80015

The Long Island Historical Miniature Collectors Society
P.O. Box 118
Wantagh, NY 11793

Virginia Company of Military Figure Collectors
11925 Smoketree Drive
Richmond, VA 23236

National Capitol Model Soldier Society Inc.
14613 Stonehouse Court
Silver Spring, MD 20905

Preparation

These kits are typical of today's World War II figures. These figures measure approximately 2 1/4" tall. They can be as large as 4" to 5" tall. The figure on the left is from Warriors Scale Models, Inc. The figure on the right is from Yanks Miniatures.

Usually you will get either painting instructions or a photograph to follow. Study these carefully.

Basic tools for clean-up and preparation of figures. These include fine sandpaper, miniature files, a small saw blade or hobby saw blade, hobby knife, and miniature twist drill.

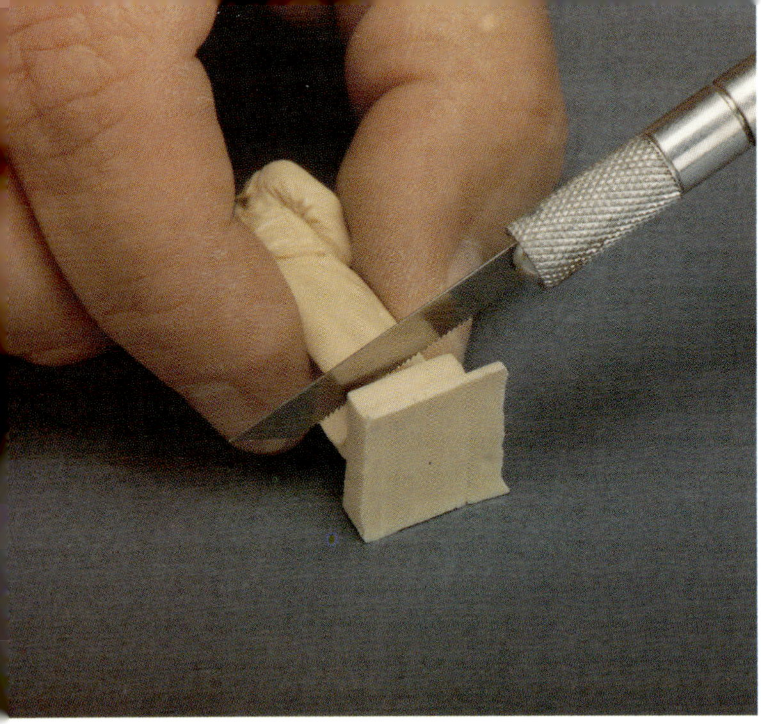

Using the miniature saw blade, remove the large plugs from the component parts.

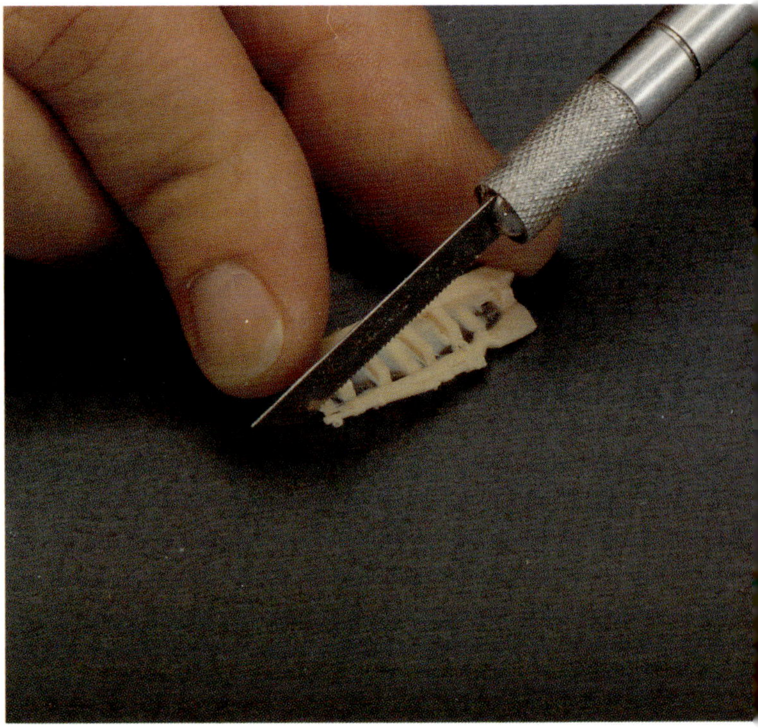

Pay particular attention to delicate parts such as the end of the barrel on this rifle.

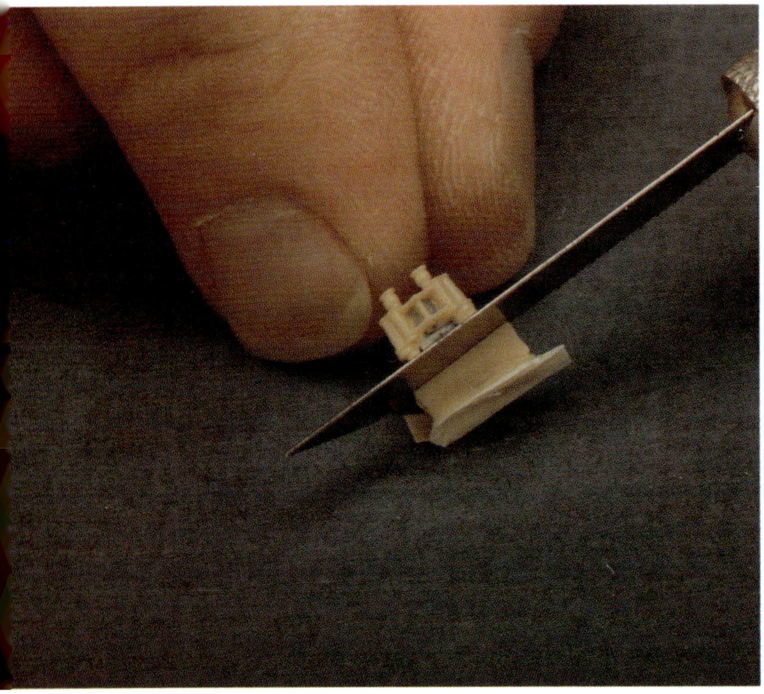

Be careful when removing the plugs from smaller parts such as these binoculars.

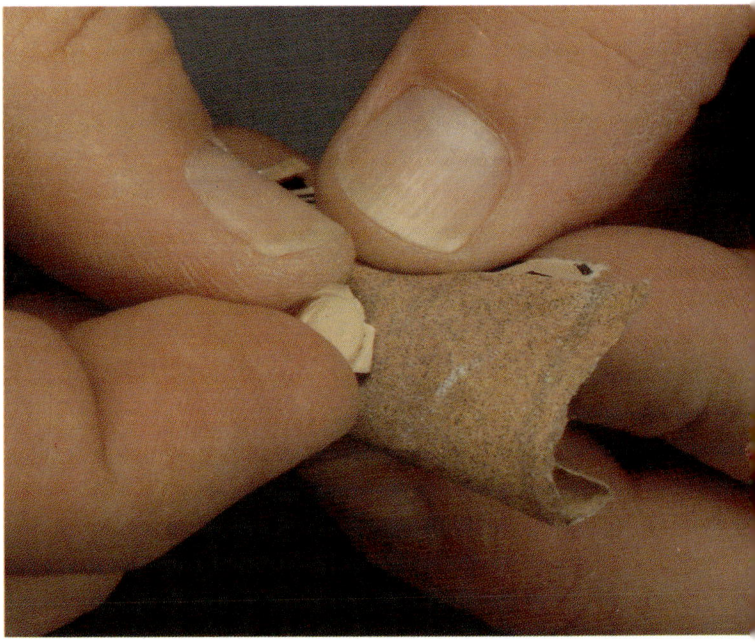

After removal of the plug, use fine hobby sandpaper to finish and remove any remaining flash.

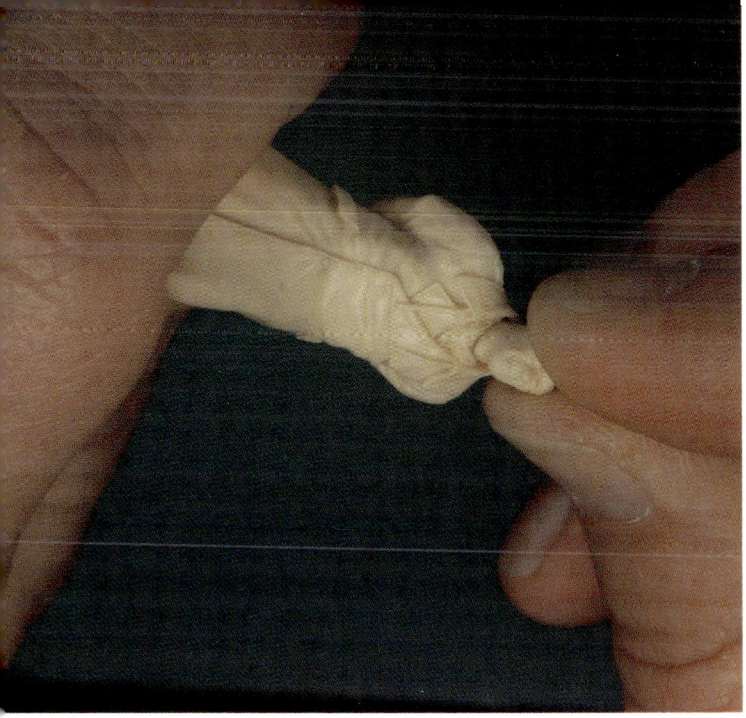

Test fit the parts as you go.

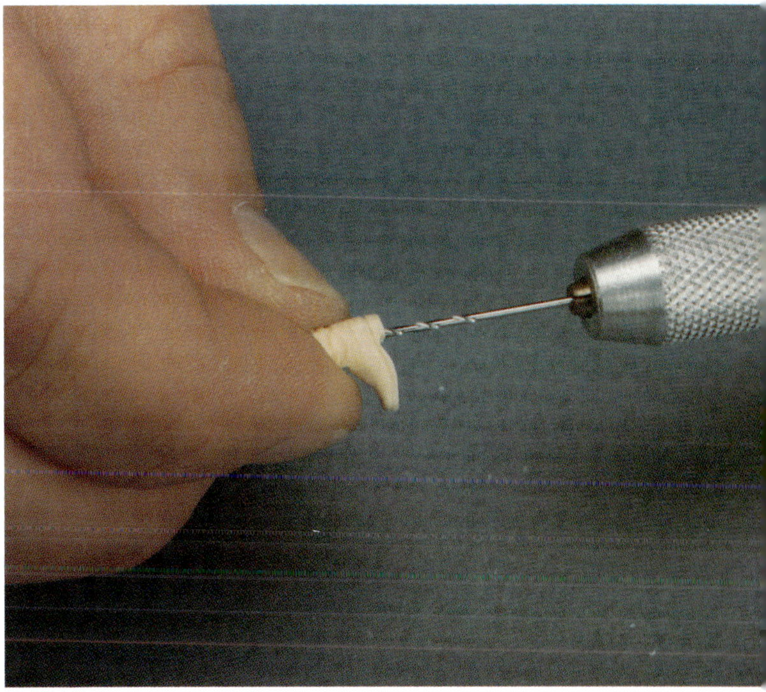

The next step is to drill a hole through the bottom of the foot deep enough to accommodate a piece of wire that will be used to secure the figure to the base.

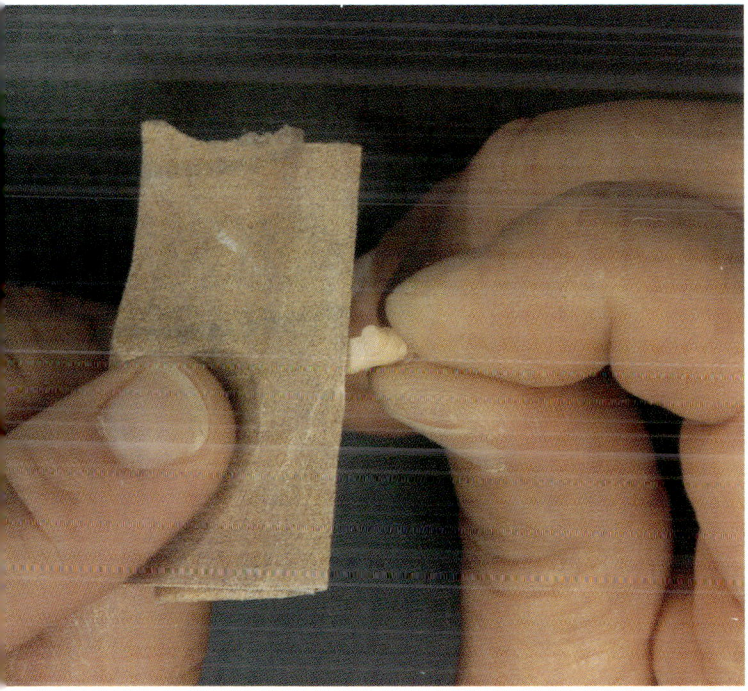

There are two basic approaches to mounting the figures to their bases. The first approach involves first smoothing off the bottom of the feet.

Two effective types of glue for use when assembling a miniature are Epoxy and Cyanoacrylate. The cyanoacrylate glues work well with resin figures. The five minute Epoxy glue works well with heavier metal figures. There are varying drying times for different formulas of cyanoacrylate glues. The slower drying, gap filling formulas are very effective on resin parts.

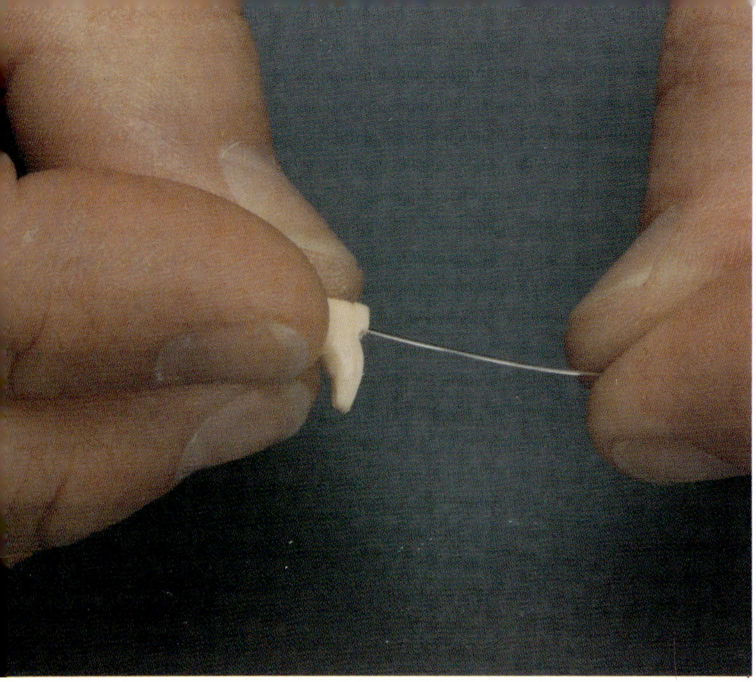

Using cyanoacrylate glue, glue a small metal rod into the hole you just drilled. This will allow you to permanently attach the figure to your display base.

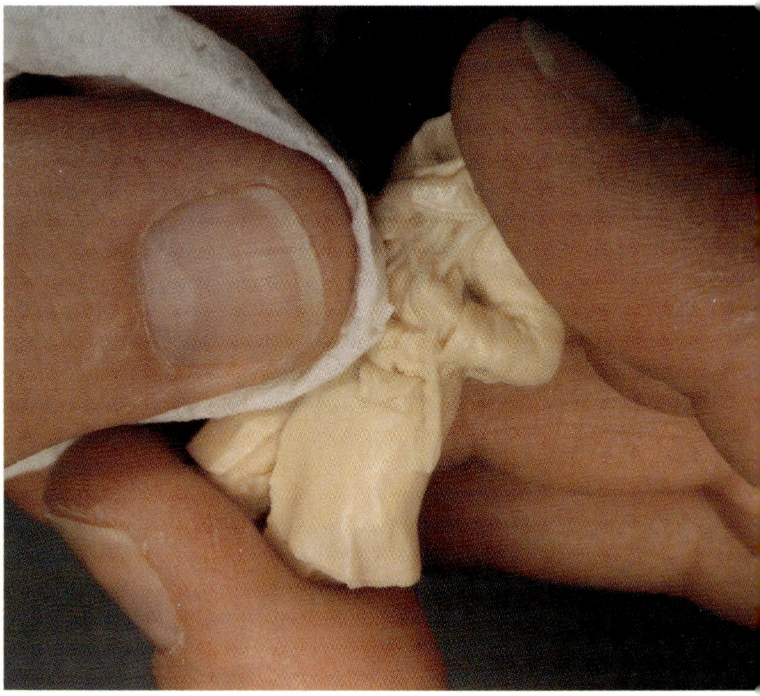

After your final clean up is finished, you may wish to wash the components in mild detergent to remove any mold release.

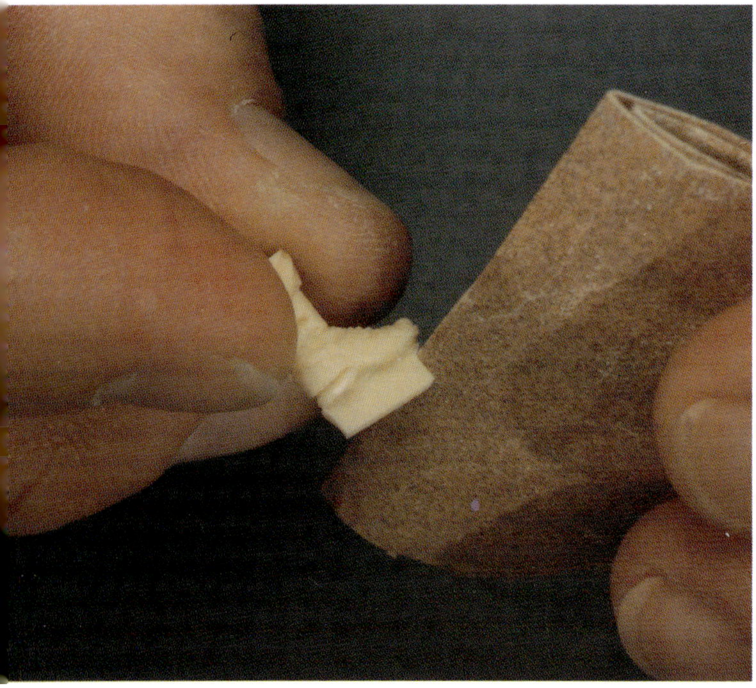

The second approach is to leave part of the plug on the bottom of one or both of the feet. This plug will be surrounded by glue when you attach it to your display base and then hidden by your ground work.

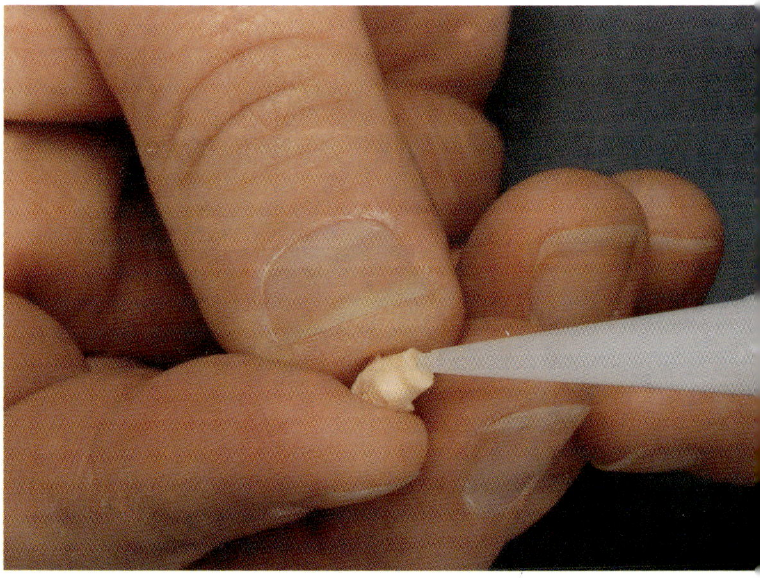

Apply glue to the component pieces and begin assembly. You may prefer to leave some pieces separate until they have been painted, especially items such as canteens, knives, etc.

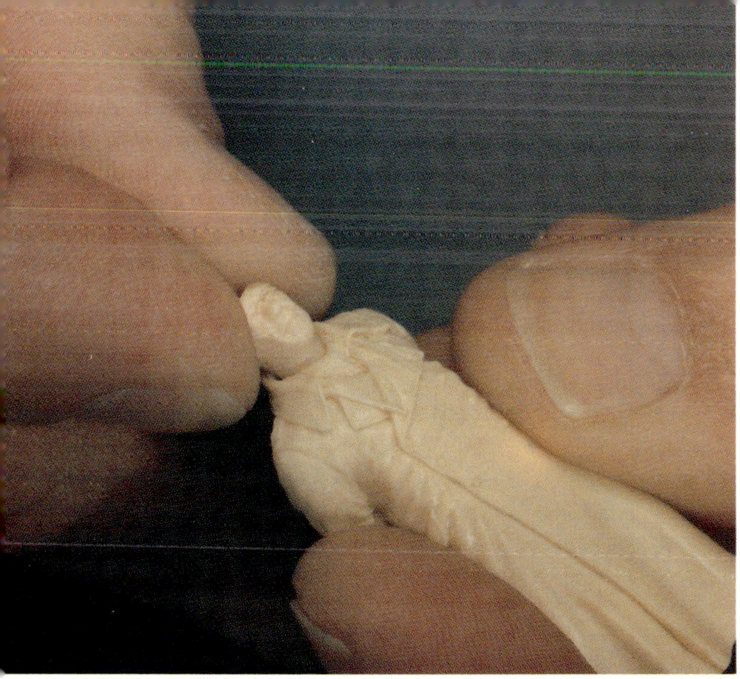

Assembling the parts, making sure to check for proper alignment and fit.

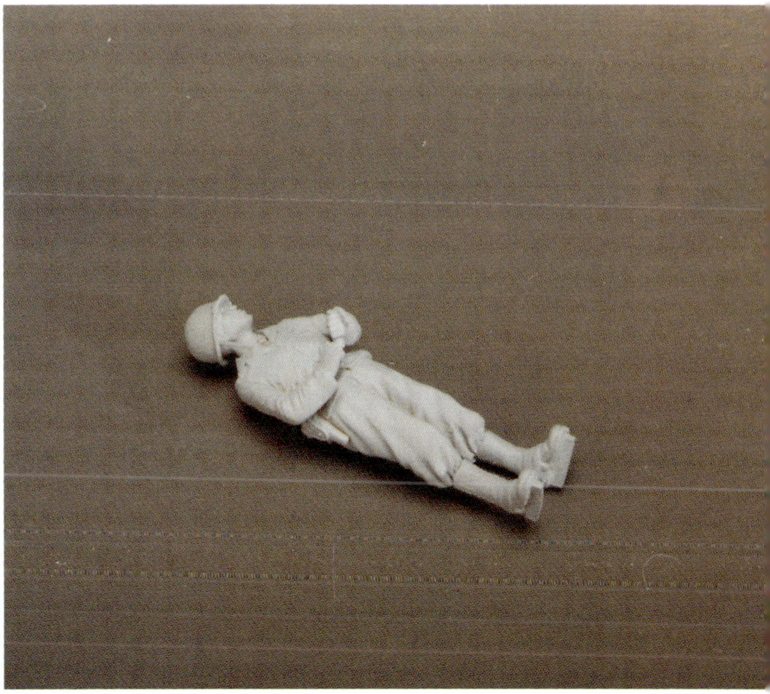

A completely assembled and primed figure of an American G.I.

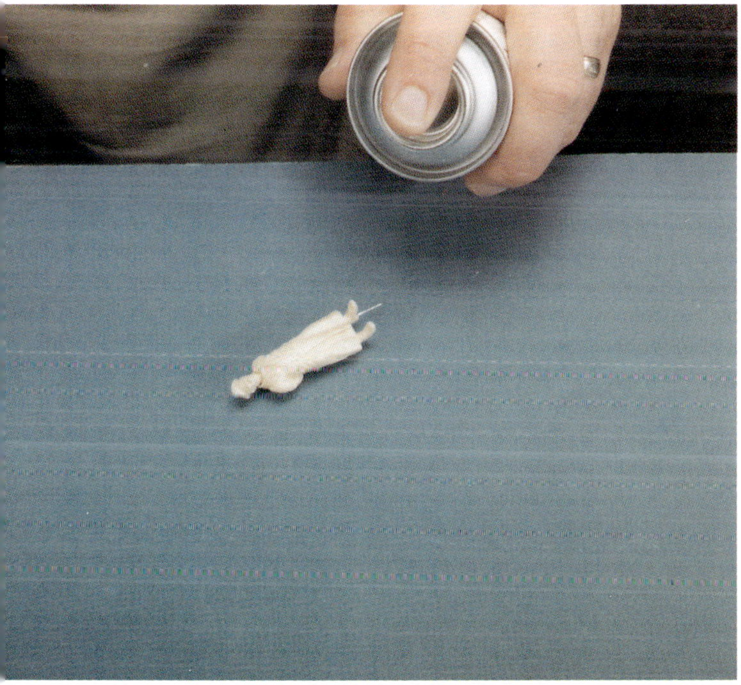

Next, prime the figure with a good quality figure primer. Allow to dry thoroughly.

I have mounted the figure on a temporary work base to facilitate painting. The figure will be transferred to a permanent display base as the project nears completion.

Painting Flesh Tones

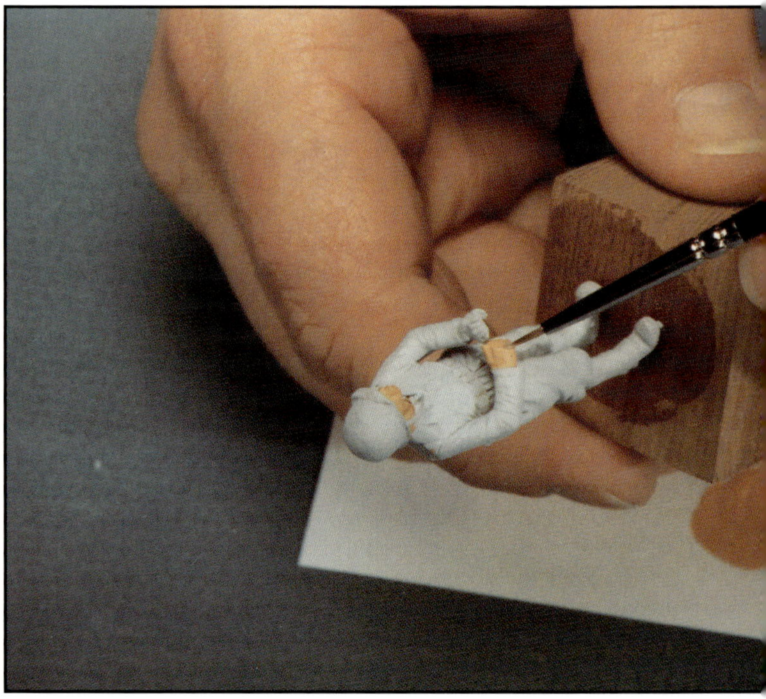

Also undercoat any exposed skin such as the hand on this figure. Let this undercoat dry thoroughly.

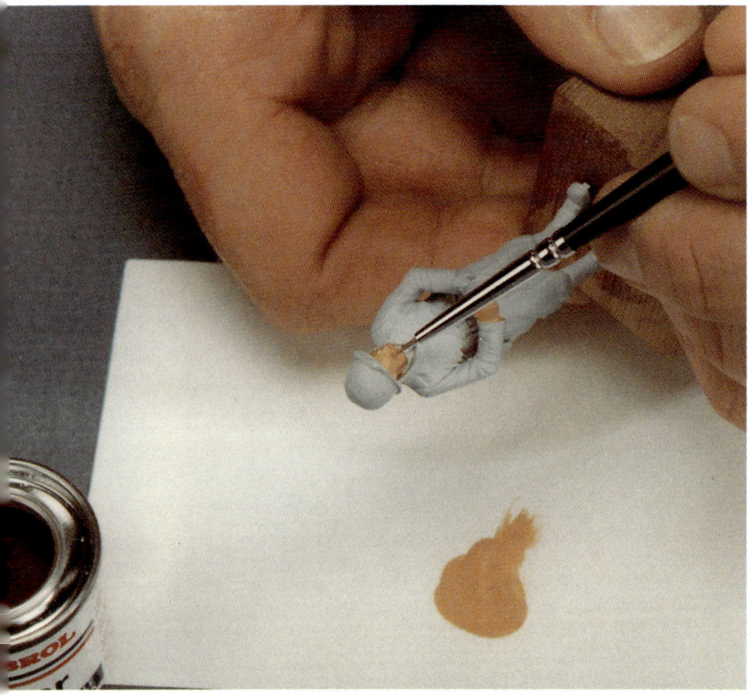

Undercoat the primed figure's face with either acrylic or enamel hobby paint.

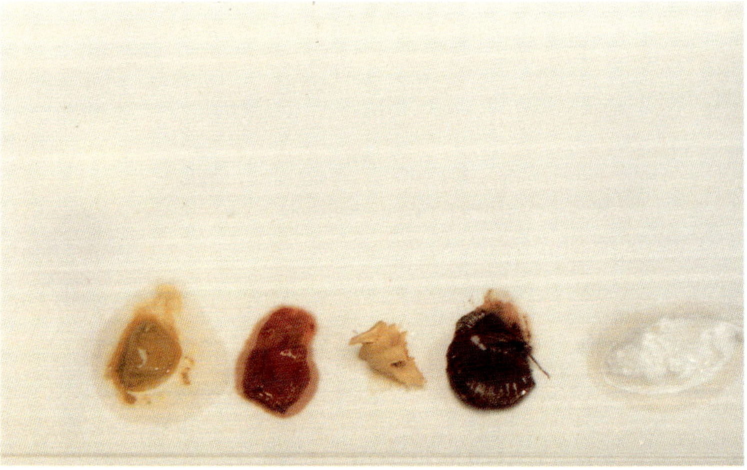

Switching to artist's oils for highlights and shadows, I mix Titanium White, Burnt Sienna or Mars Brown, Cadmium Yellow, Cadmium Red, and Yellow Ochre to create Caucasian skin tones.

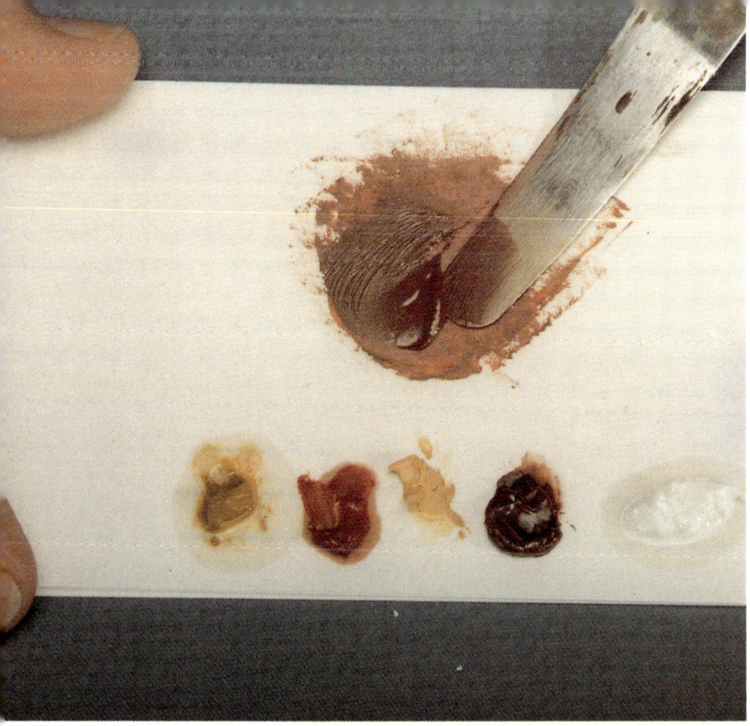

While this is not an exact science, mix the Cadmium Red, both yellows, and a small amount of brown together and then begin to add the white.

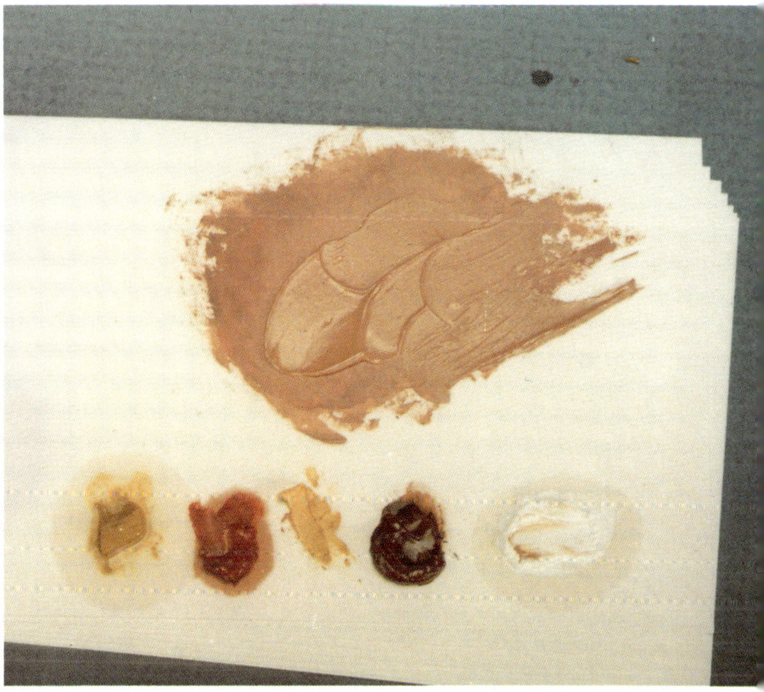

The finished basic flesh tone. From this color we will lighten and darken to paint the exposed flesh on our figures. Experiment with this basic flesh tone until you achieve a color that is pleasing to your eye.

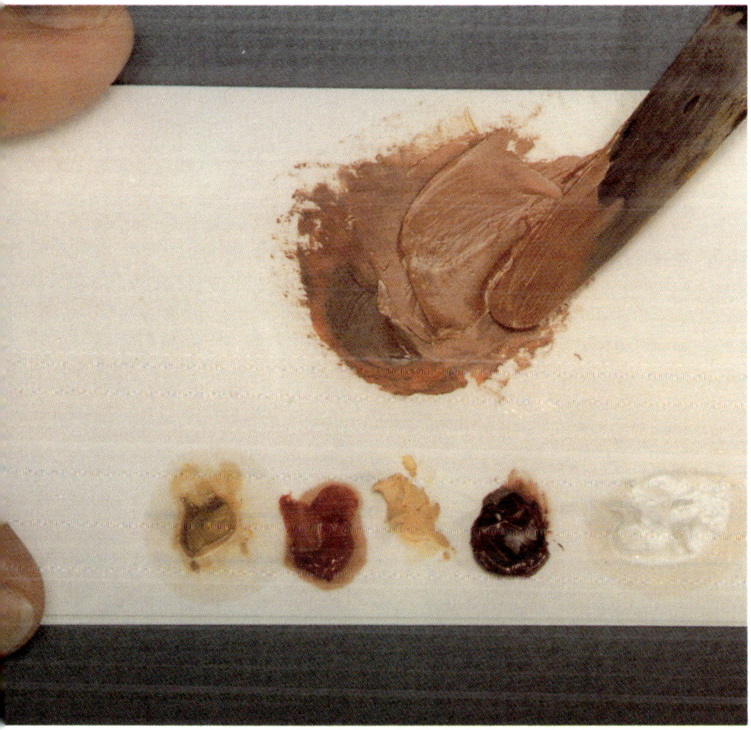

Adding the white.

Apply Burnt Sienna into the recessed areas along the smile line, underneath the bottom side of the nose, and under the lower lip.

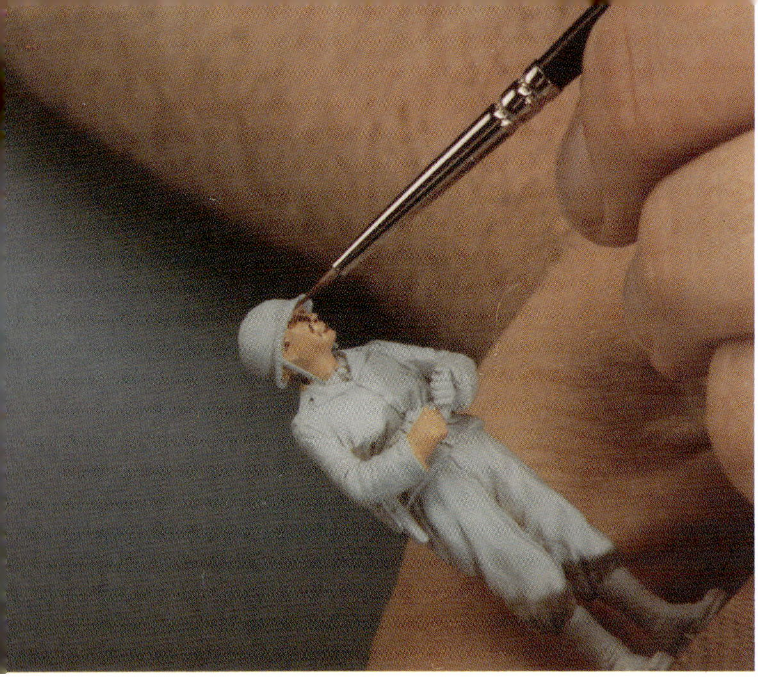

Continue to place Burnt Sienna along the sides of the nose, underneath the brow line, and around the eye sockets.

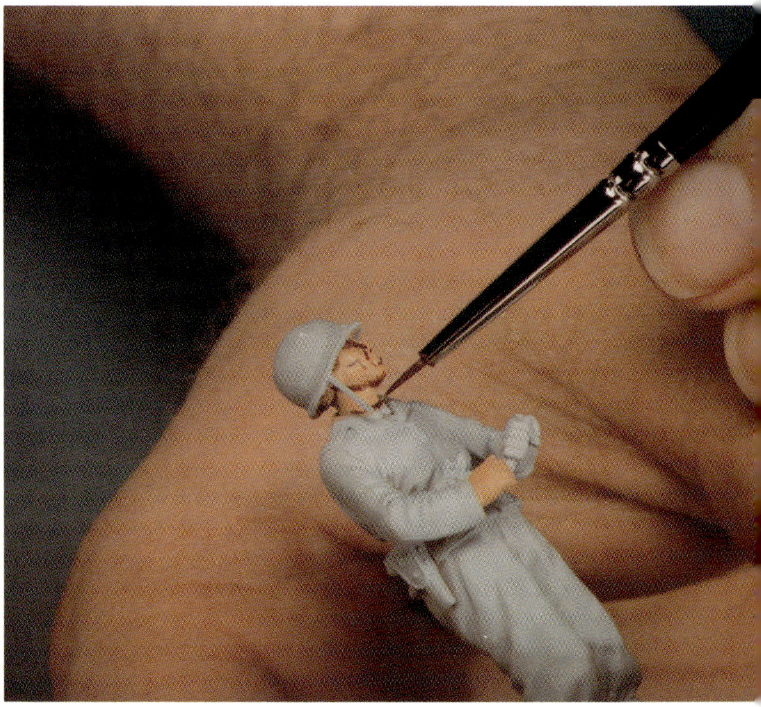

Apply this dark brown color in a triangular fashion in the hollows of the cheeks and put a thin line of brown where the neck meets the shirt.

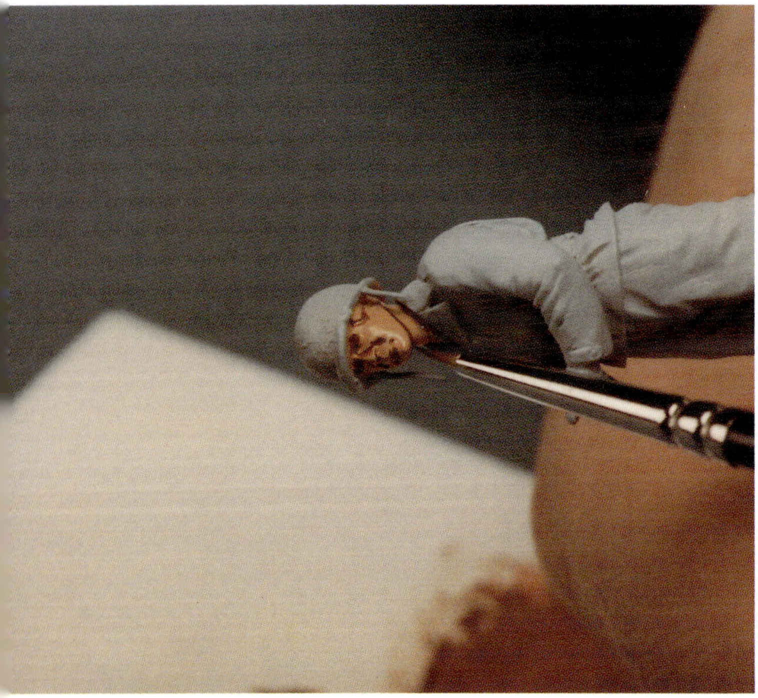

Also place this color along the lower jaw line and outline the hair, continuing around to the back of the ear.

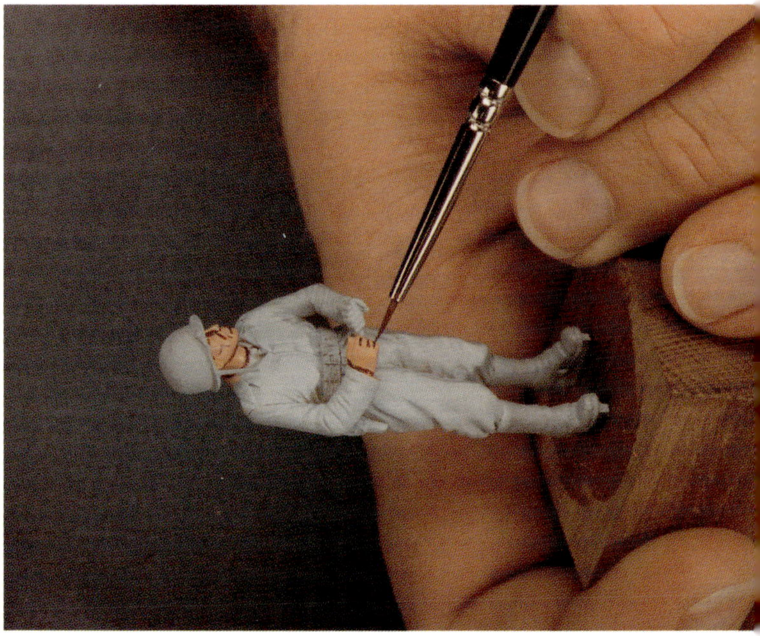

Locate any recessed areas on the hands, arms, or legs where there is flesh showing. Place the dark brown color into these areas.

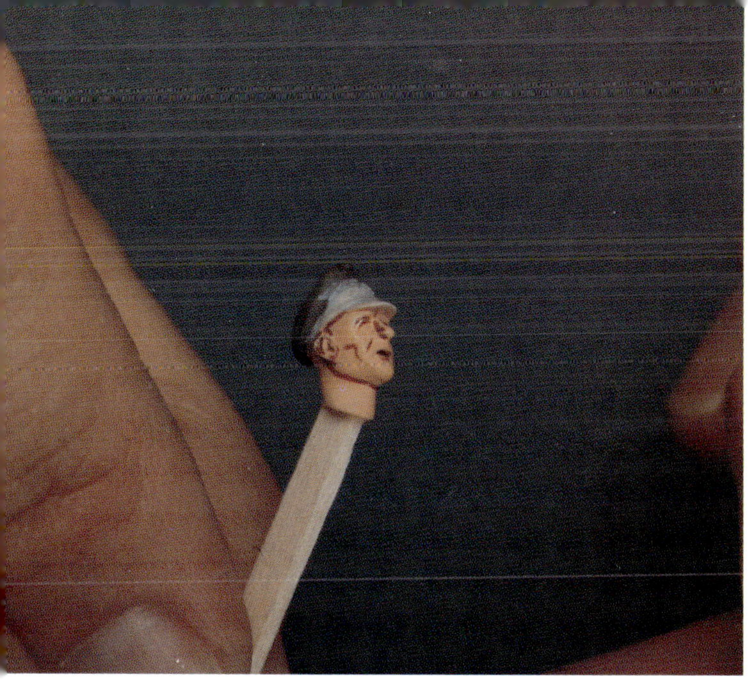

In the case of a figure with an open mouth such as the head shown here, also darken the opened area of the mouth. Note that I have also darkened in the crevices of the ear and along the cap line, where the cap meets the skin.

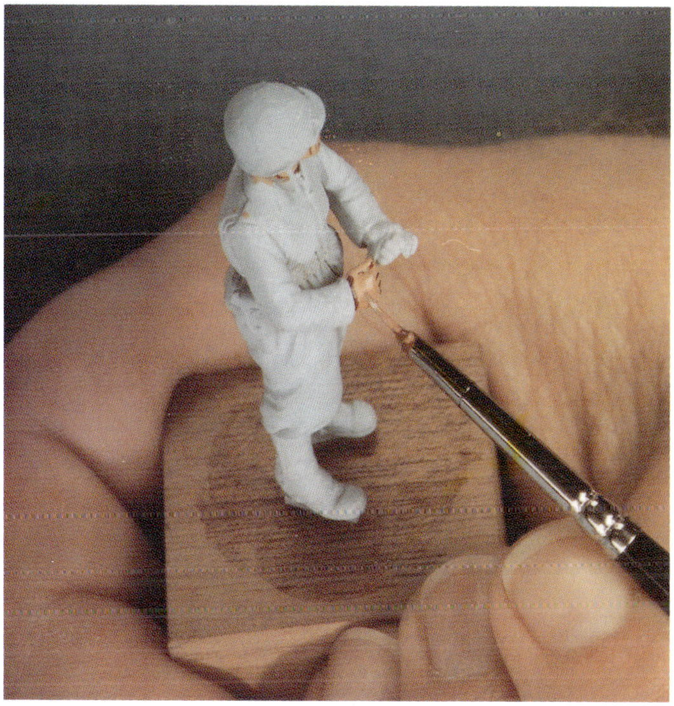

Apply the middle flesh tone to the skin. Bring it right up to the shadow lines.

The shadow colors have been applied. Keep in mind that there may be additional areas that demand the shadow color such as the cleft in the chin.

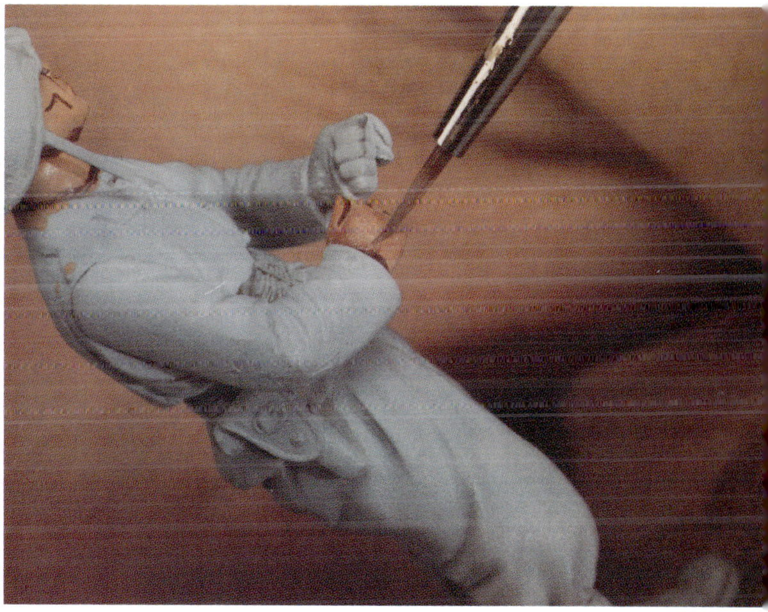

Using a dabbing or pecking motion, soften the demarcation line between the middle and shadow colors. Be careful not to draw the shadow color too far out into the area of the middle flesh tone.

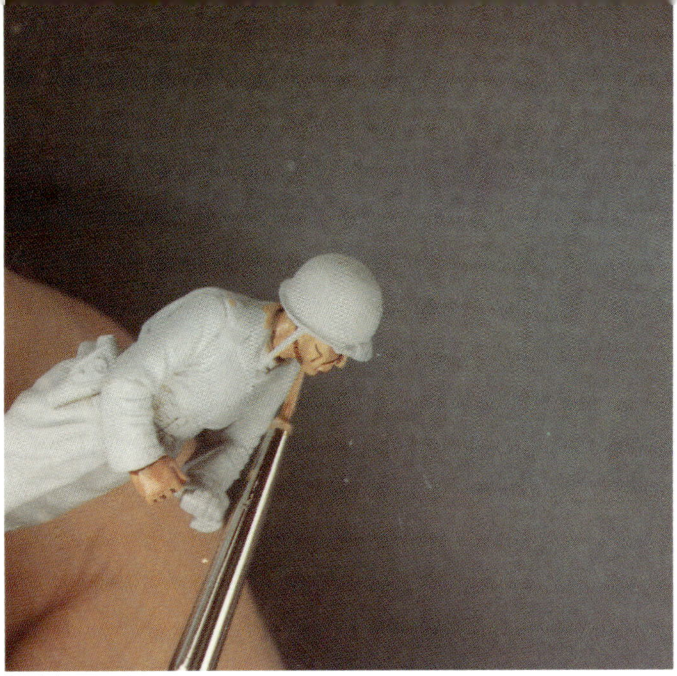

Continuing to apply the middle color to the face.

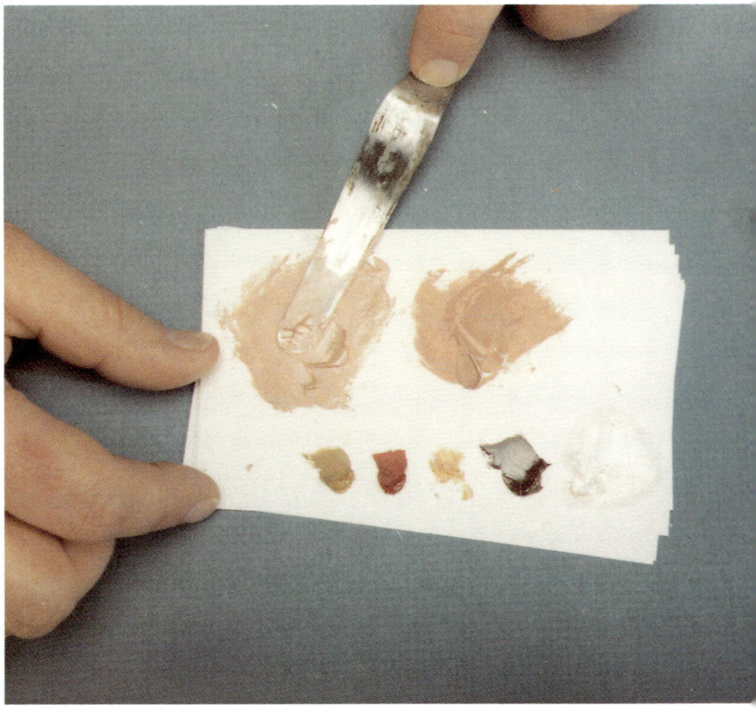

For a highlight color mix additional white and a small amount of Cadmium Yellow to the flesh color.

Blend the middle color and the shadows together.

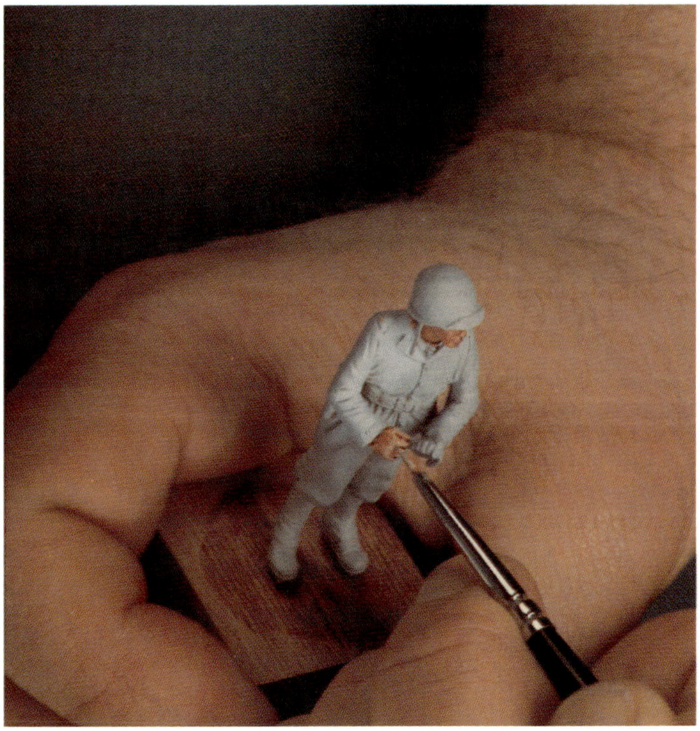

Apply this highlight color to specific areas such as the tops of the knuckles, the leading edge of the fingers, and any other raised area.

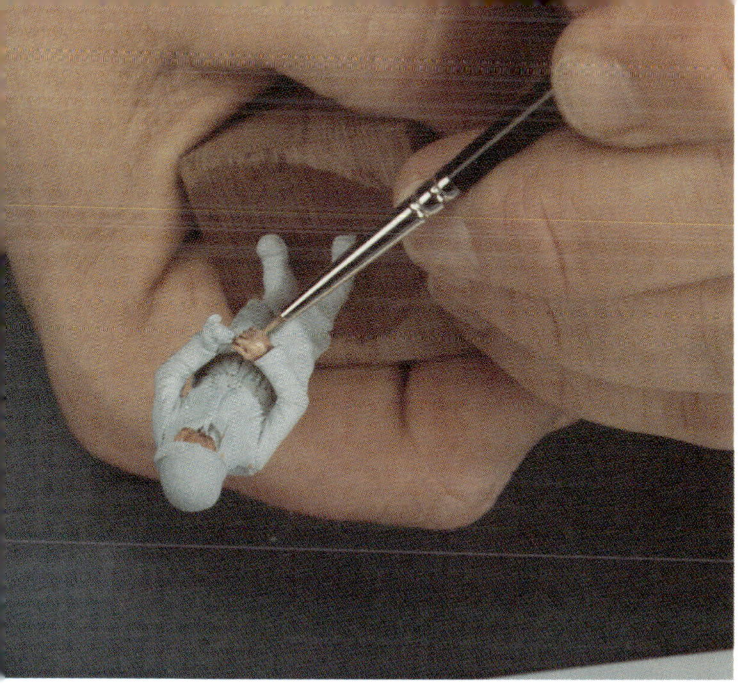

Soften these areas using the dabbing motion. Be very careful not to overwork the area or you will lose your contrast from light to dark.

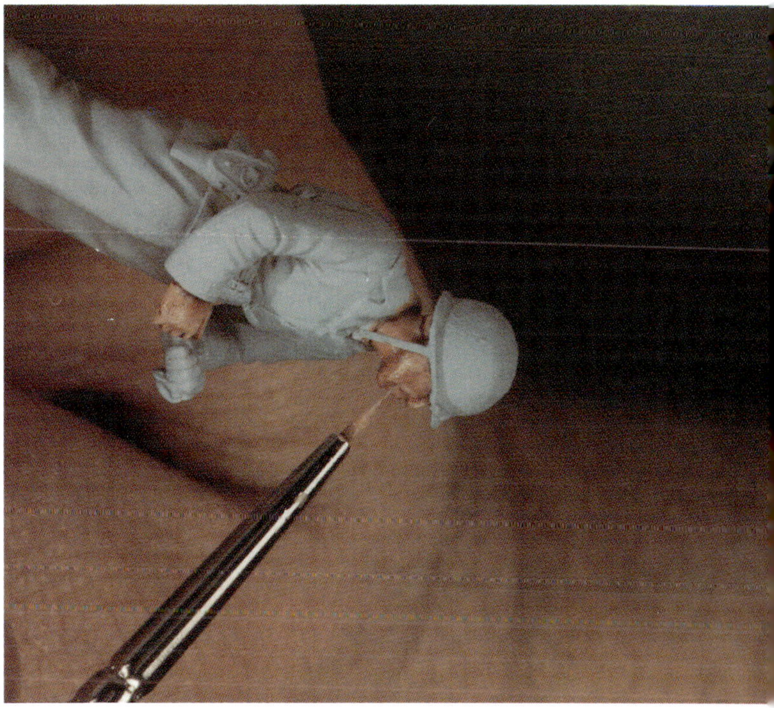

Blend as before using the dabbing motion.

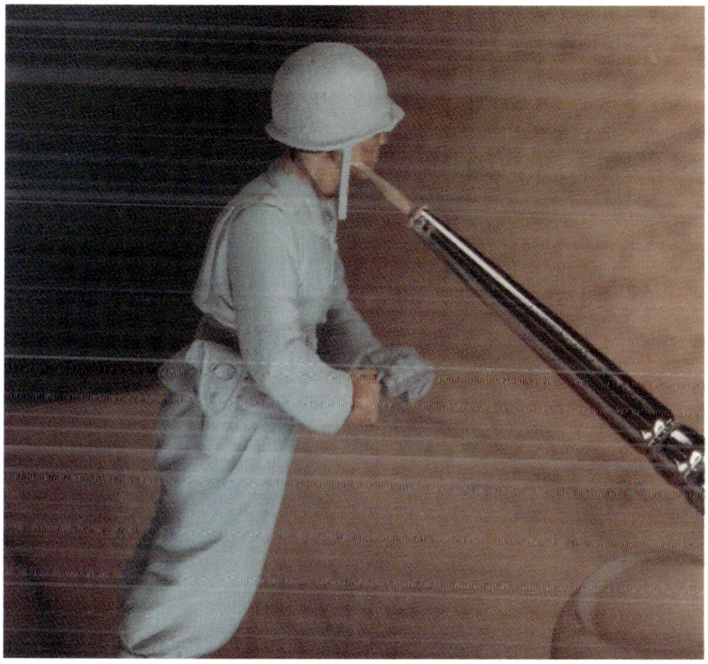

Continue to add the highlight color to the face along the upper jaw line, the top of the nose, the top of the ears, cheek bones, the front of the chin, between the nose and the upper lip, and along the top of the ridge created by the smile lines.

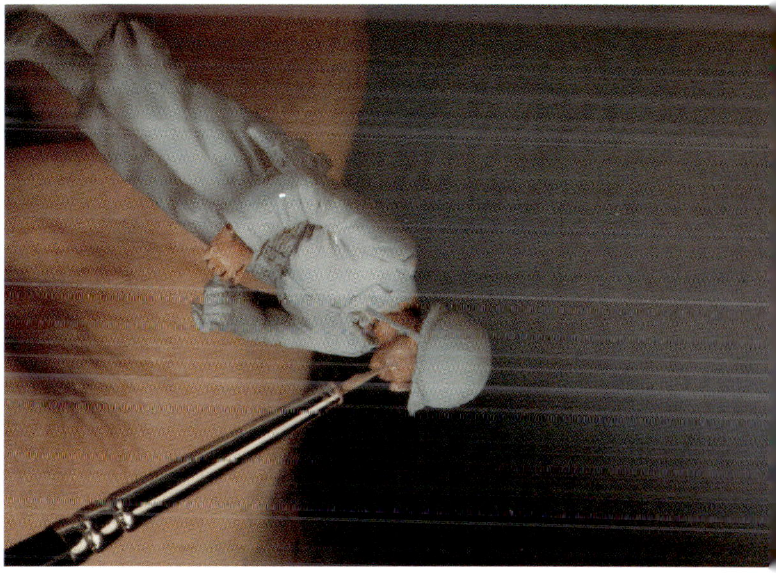

After your highlight blending is completed, you may find it necessary to reinforce some of your shadow colors if you have overblended on the face. As a final touch, add a small amount of red to the middle flesh color and apply this to the lower lip. Add highlight color to the lower eye lids. At this scale, all that is needed to finish the eyes is a dark line of Burnt Umber to indicate squinting eyes.

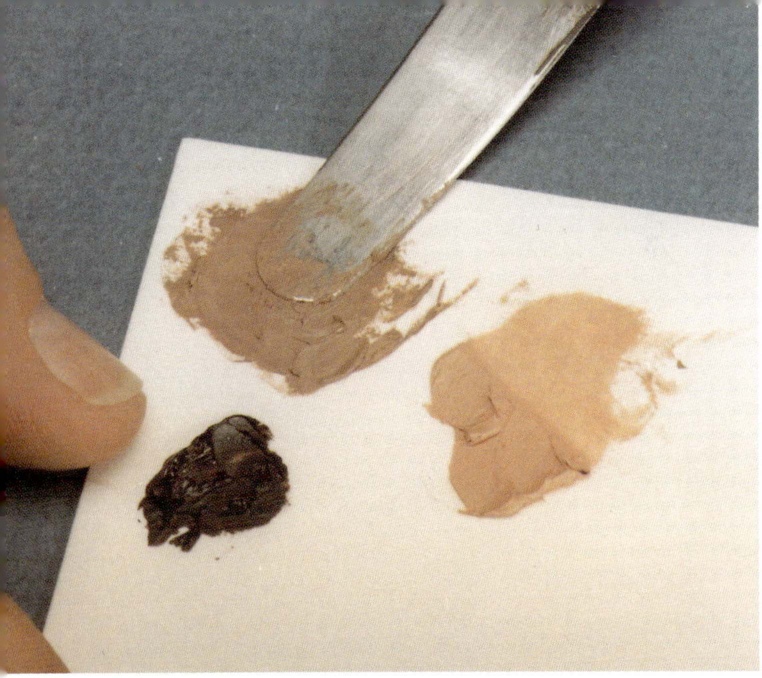

If you wish to create a five o'clock shadow add a small amount of Burnt Umber to the middle flesh color.

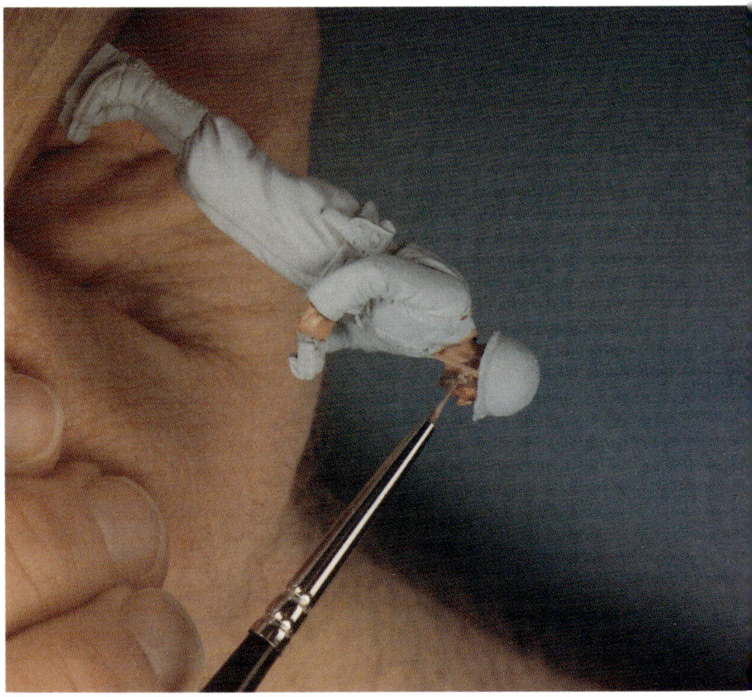

Next, place a small amount of your middle flesh color starting in the middle of the jaw.

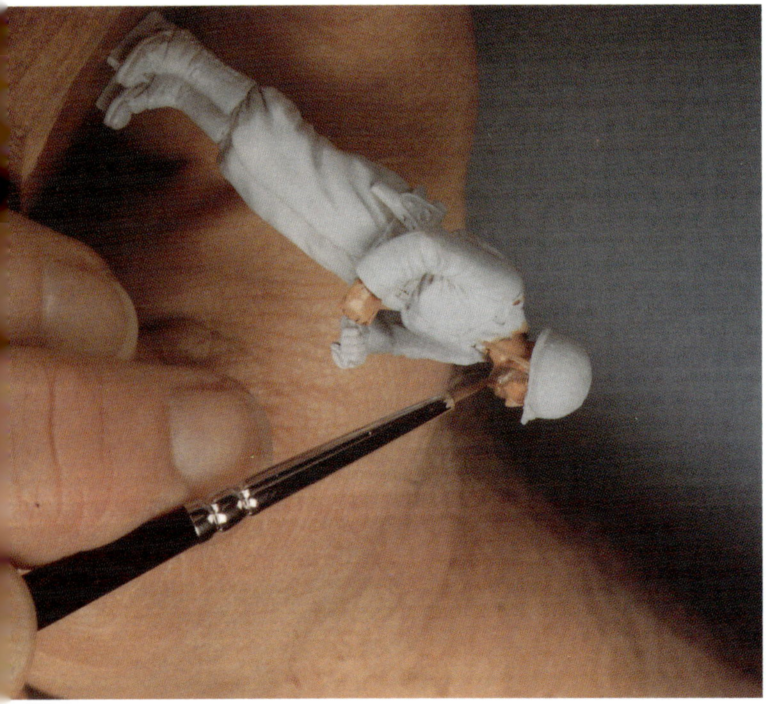

Apply this color along the beard line.

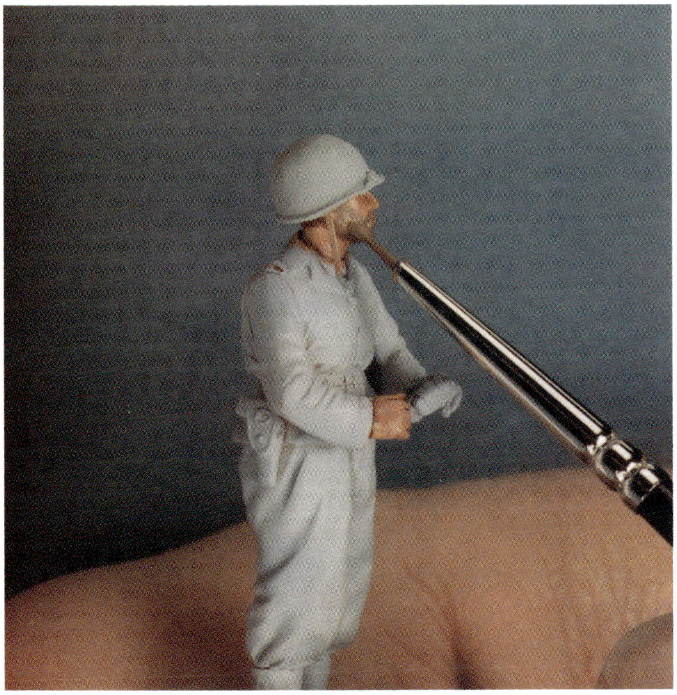

Again using the dabbing motion, soften the line between the five o'clock shadow color and the flesh tone.

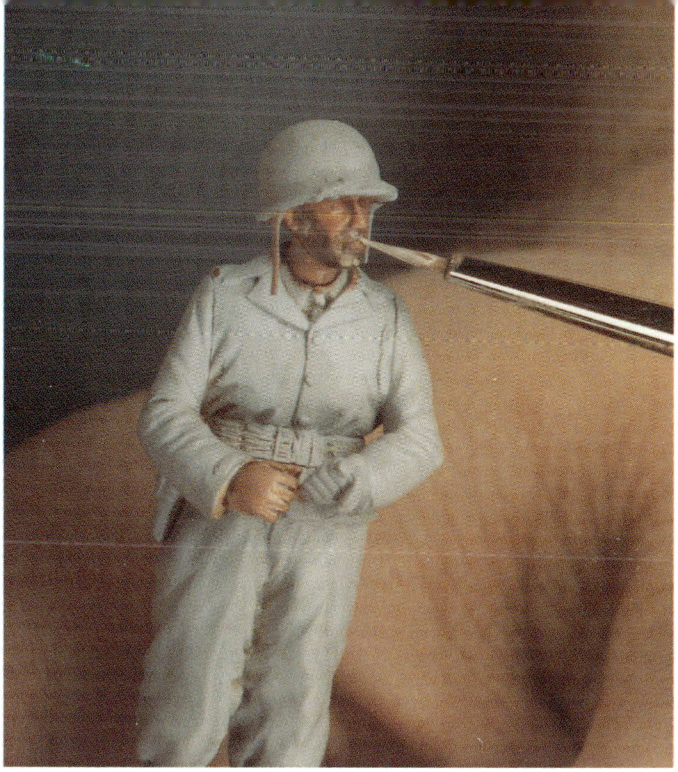

To create a highlight for the five o'clock shadow, use the flesh tone highlight color. Place a small amount on the end of the chin, a dot on each side of the area between the upper lip and the nose, and again on the jaw next to the ear.

The finished G.I.'s face.

Gently blend these highlight colors. Be careful and don't overwork these highlights.

Here are good examples of finished arms and faces. Again notice the scruffiness of the American G.I. in combat uniform compared to the clean shaven German.

Uniforms

There are many good reference sources available today with which to check colors and details for accuracy.

Now we are ready to start painting uniforms. Begin by undercoating the primed areas using enamel or water based paints of a color that closely matches the color of the uniform—such as olive drab for the helmet on this American soldier…

…or field gray for this German infantryman. Continue to undercoat all remaining uniform and equipment items on your figure.

This is a completely undercoated figure. We are now ready to use oil paints.

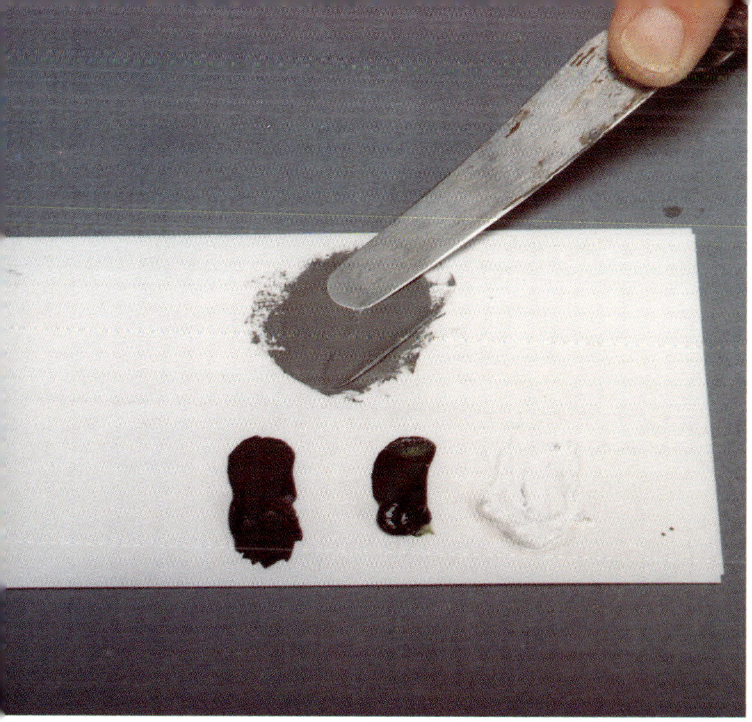

Start by mixing a middle color that closely approximates your undercoat color. Even though this is German field gray, the basic mixing technique will apply to any color you are creating. The three colors used in the German field gray are Ivory Black, Titanium White, and a small amount of Sap Green.

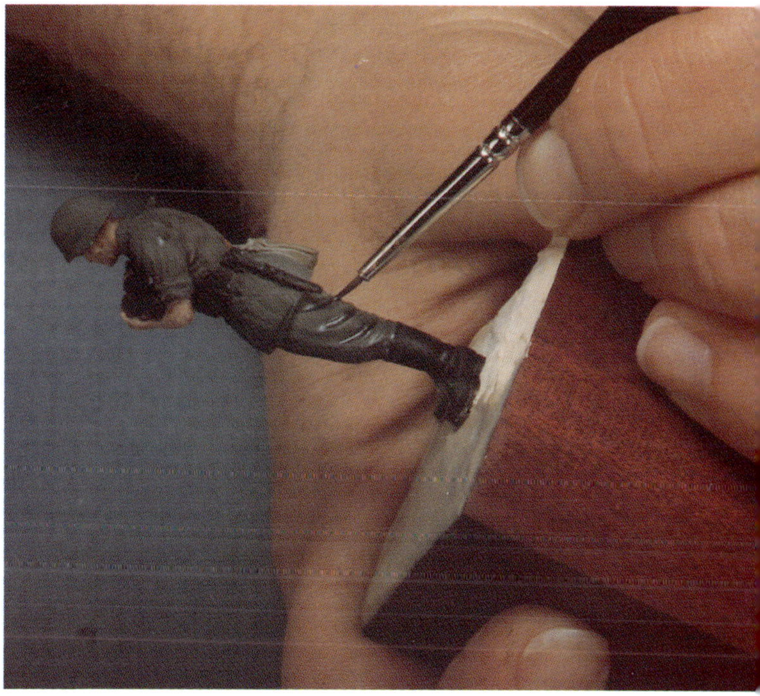

Apply the shadow color to the recessed areas, such as the folds of the uniform.

The highlight and the shadow colors are created by adding either white (highlights) or black (shadows) to the middle color.

Outline any areas such as pockets or pleats.

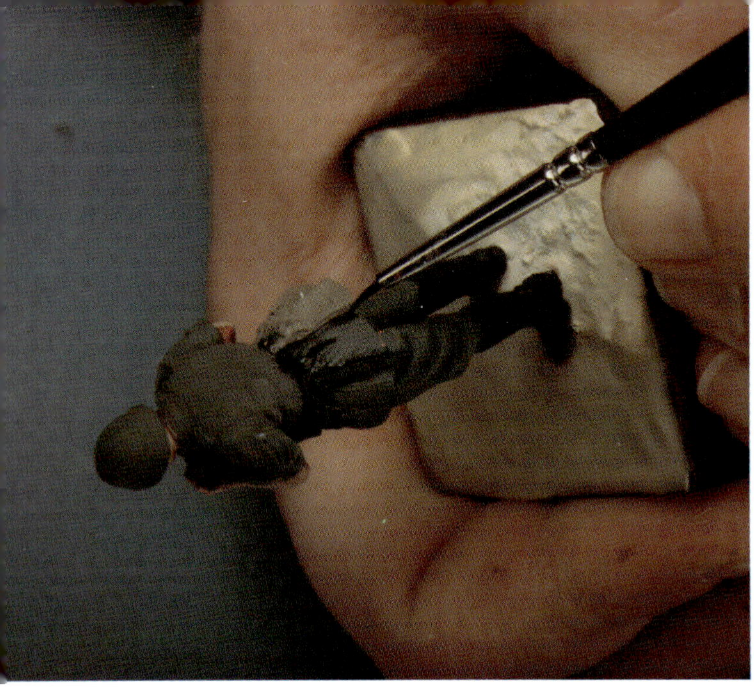

Continue outlining around equipment items such as the bread bag on this German soldier. Also outline where the belts or straps touch the uniform.

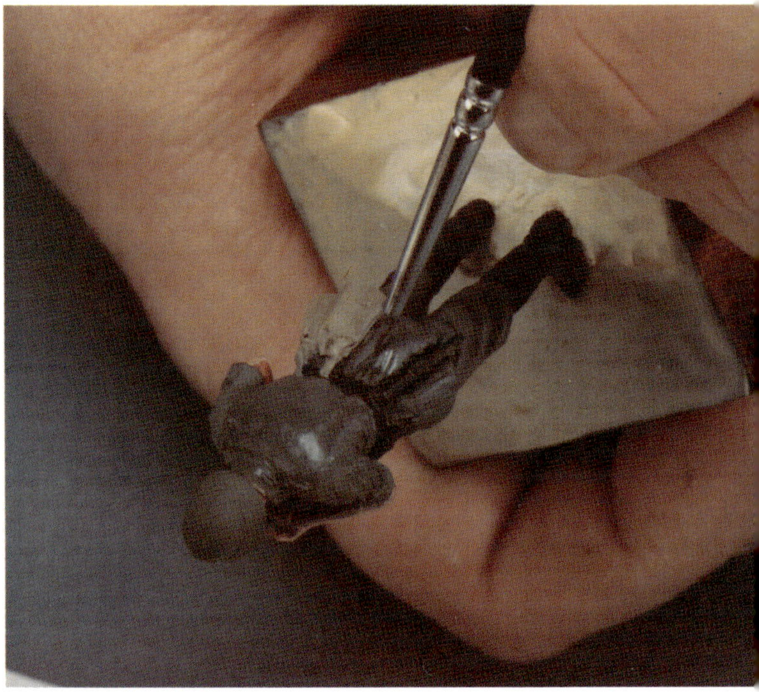

Using our tried-and-true dabbing motion, soften the line between the shadow and middle colors. Keep in mind this applies to any color uniform you are painting.

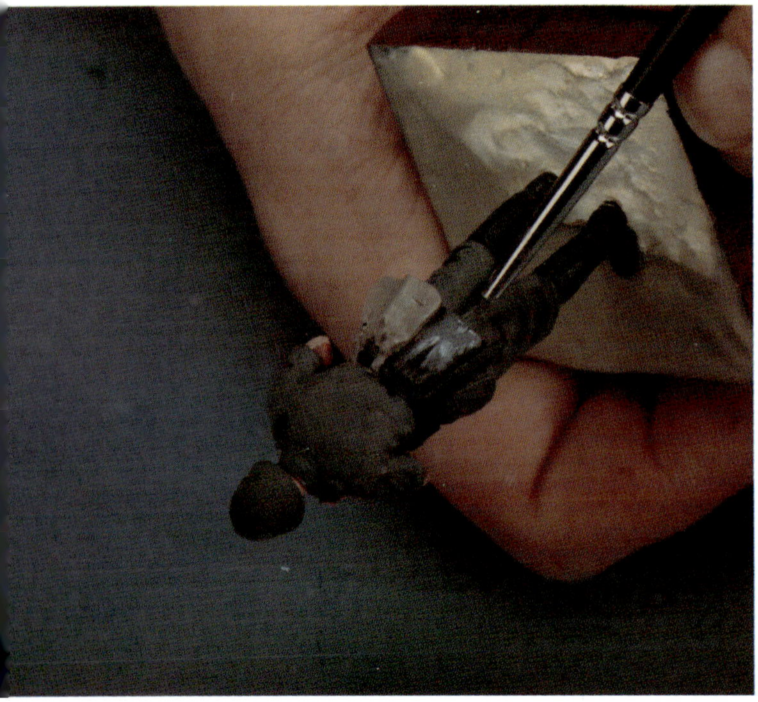

Now apply the middle color to the figure, bringing it up to the shadow color.

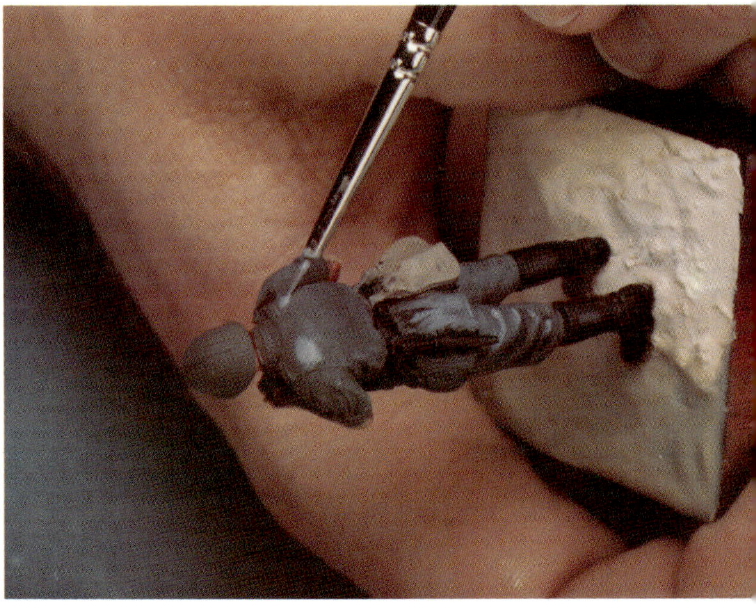

The next step is to apply our highlight color to raised portions of the uniform. These will include the tops of folds, the upper area of the shoulders, the tops of pleats, etc.

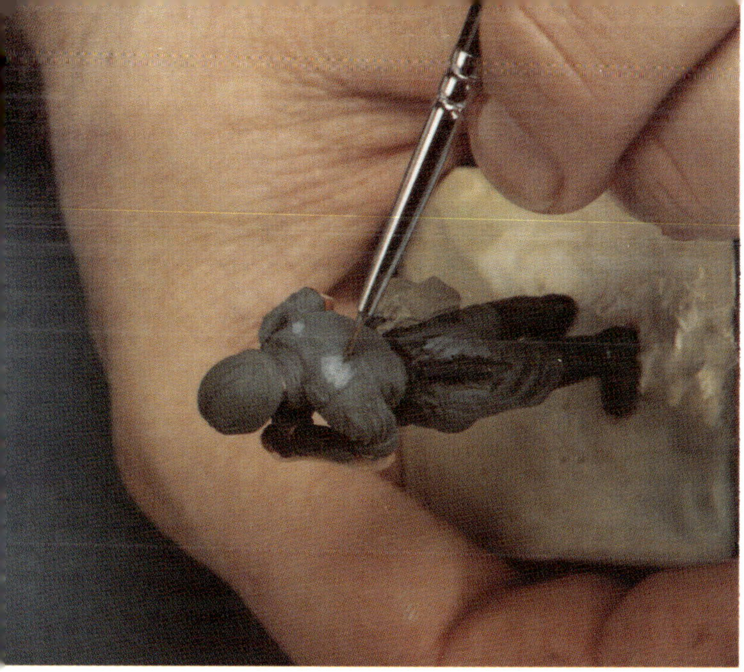

Gently soften these highlights.

To create a soiled look, add Burnt Umber to your highlight uniform color.

Apply this dirty color to areas that you wish to show additional wear-and-tear. These areas usually include the front of the pants near the knees, the seat of the pants, and the pant cuffs. Be creative! The more you apply, the dirtier your soldier will be.

Mix additional white for a highlight for our dirty areas. Apply this highlight to the dirty areas just as we have applied highlights to the rest of the uniform.

This mechanic figure's pants are a fine example of the dirtying techniques.

Keep in mind that when painting black uniforms you need to ensure that your highlights do not become too light. If this happens, you will wind up with a uniform that is no longer black.

In the case of this German soldier dressed in black, I used Ivory Black, plus a small amount of Yellow Ochre to create the middle black uniform color. Additional black has been added to create our shadow color. Add to the middle color additional Yellow Ochre to create our highlight color. You may also use white in place of Yellow Ochre, giving you shades of gray.

These Germans are wearing shades of Olive Green. Mix Burnt Umber, Sap Green, and Yellow Ochre to arrive at your middle color. Add Burnt Umber to the middle color for a shadow color and add Yellow Ochre to the middle color to create a highlight. Apply these to the figure as we did with the field gray uniform color in three steps.

This photo demonstrates the subtle changes in color that can be achieved by mixing one of a variety of colors to a common color. The top row shows Burnt Umber mixed with Yellow Ochre on the left, Naples Yellow in the center, and White on the right. The second row demonstrates mixes Raw Umber with the same three colors. The bottom row shows the same three colors mixed with Burnt Sienna.

Notice that our walking G.I. is a study in different shades of greens and browns.

This figure's wool trousers have a middle color made by mixing Burnt Sienna and Yellow Ochre.

The highlight color is created by adding Yellow Ochre to the middle color. For a shadow color add additional Burnt Sienna.

The color for the overcoat is a bit more greenish than the pants. I have mixed Raw Umber and Yellow Ochre to create my middle color.

After adding more Yellow Ochre to make the highlight color and more Burnt Sienna for the shadow color, apply these colors using the same methods as we previously used on the German field gray uniform.

For the woolen gloves and scarf, mix Raw Umber, Sap Green, and a small amount of White for the middle color.

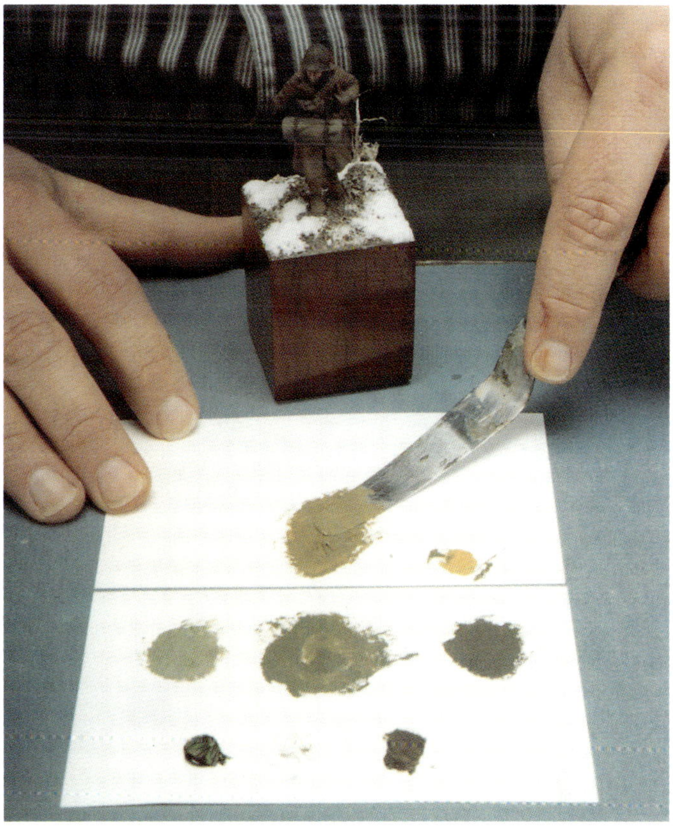

For variety I added a small amount of Yellow Ochre to the middle color that I used for the gloves and scarf and used this new color to paint the sleeping bag at the front of the figure.

Create a highlight color by mixing additional White to the middle color and a shadow color by mixing the middle color with more Raw Umber.

The sleeping bag highlight color was created with the addition of Yellow Ochre and the shadow color was created with the addition of Raw Umber.

The figure depicted here is wearing the M1941 field jacket. This was made of a beige cotton/poplin material. To mix this color combine Raw Umber, Yellow Ochre, and a small amount of Sap Green and White.

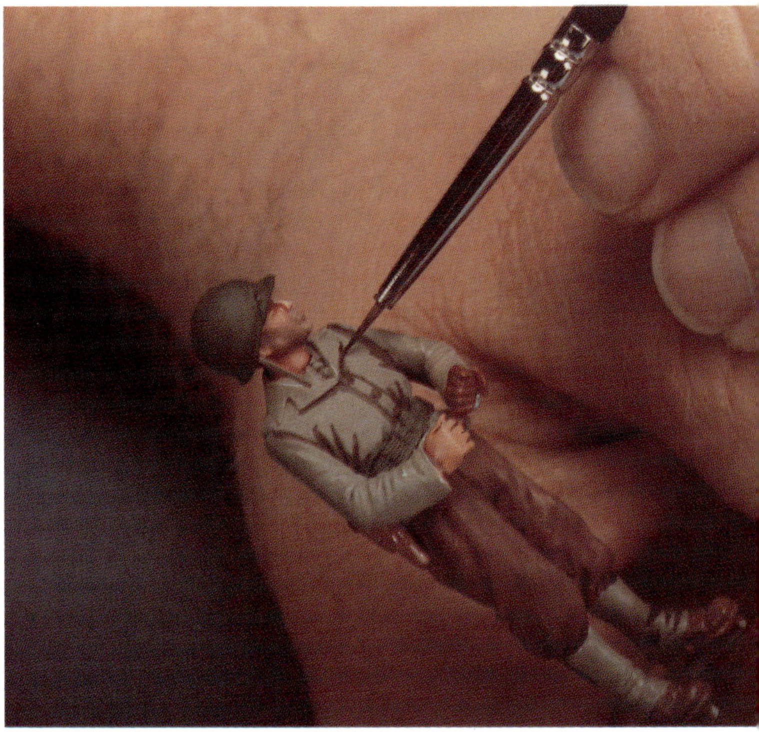

Apply the shadow color to the recessed areas in the folds along the seams where the jacket halves overlap at the buttons.

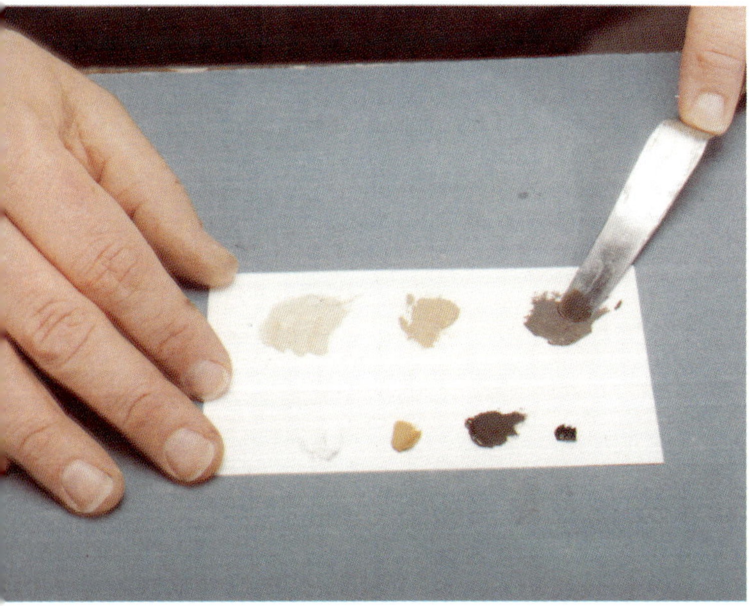

Having created the middle color we can make the highlight by adding more White, and shadow by adding more Raw Umber.

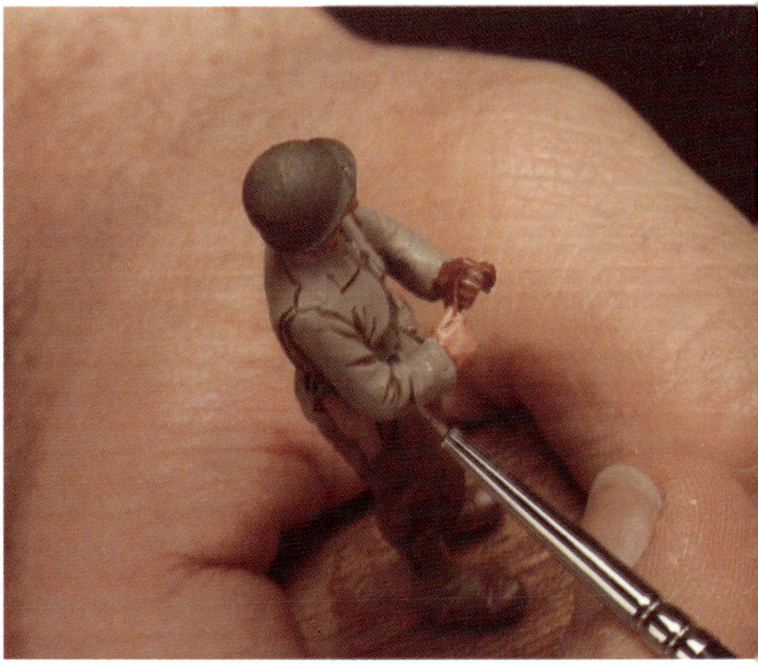

Work your way around the arms, picking out all of the folds.

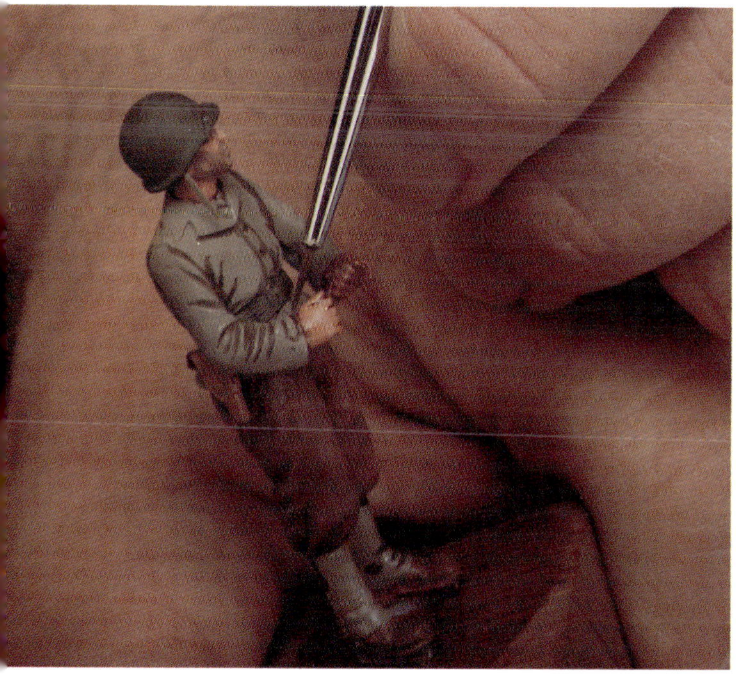

Outline the button tab on the cuffs of the jacket.

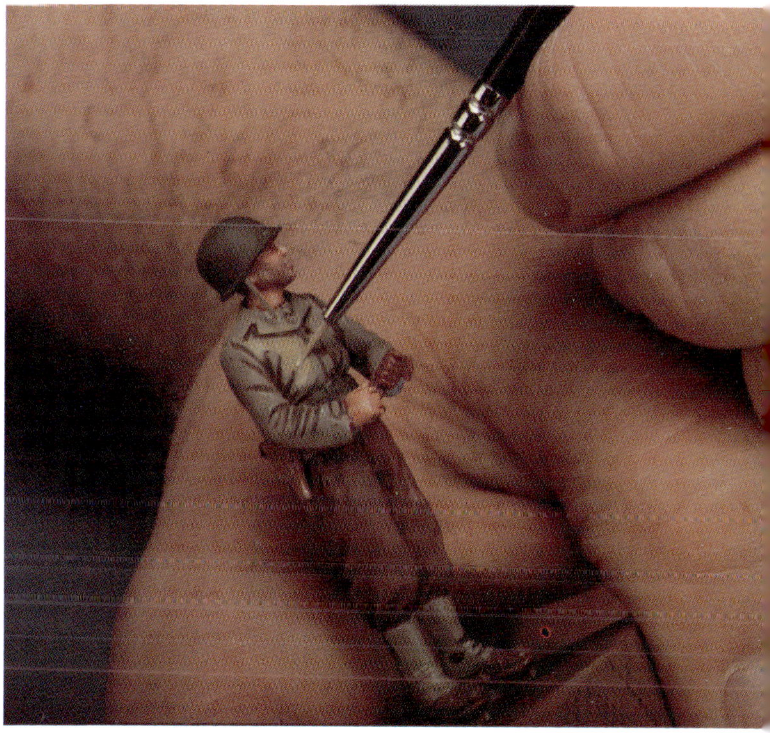

Apply the middle color to the jacket, bringing it against the shadow color you have applied.

Follow the collar line and paint the dark shadow in a thin line. Also paint a thin line at the base of the epaulet.

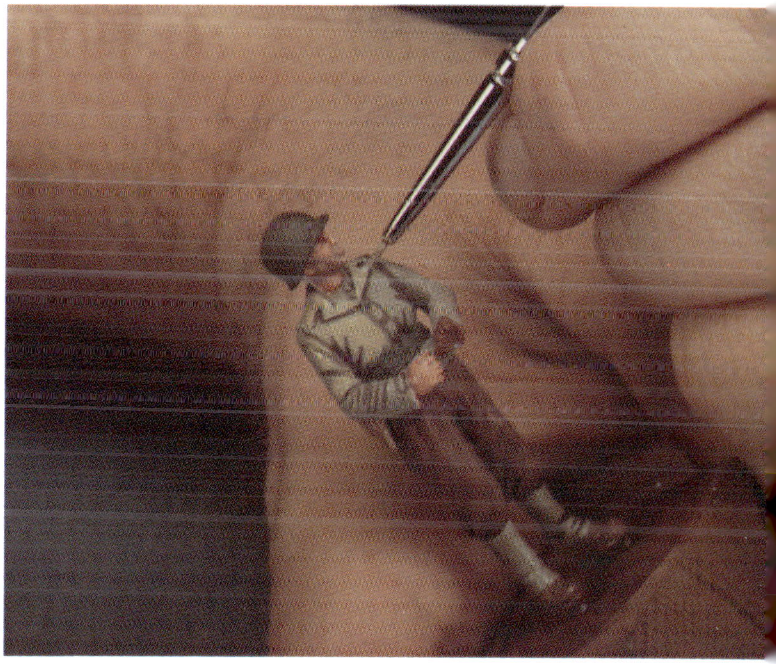

Progress.

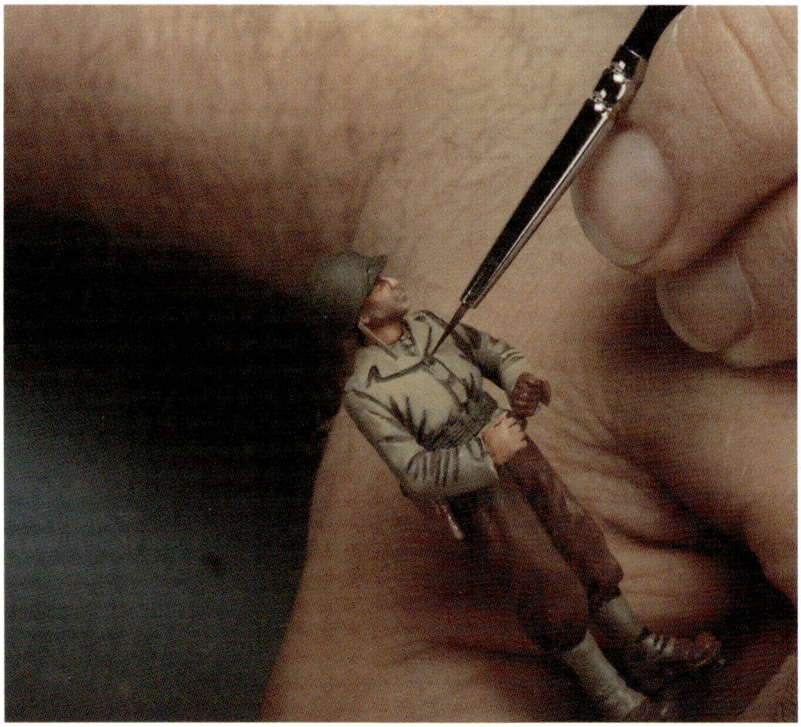

Soften the demarcation line between the middle and shadow colors.

The shadow and the middle color are now blended.

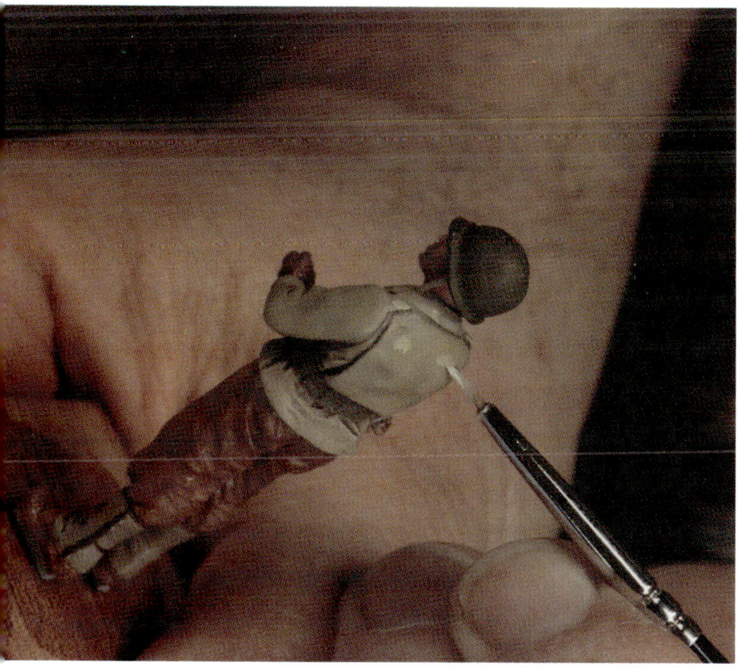

Apply the highlight colors to the jacket.

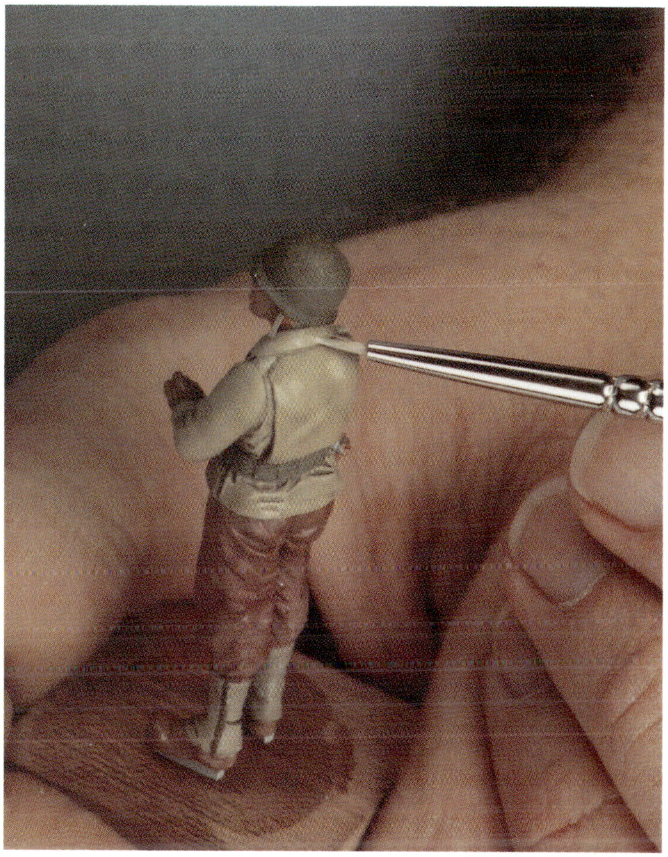

Carefully blend these highlights, using the dabbing motion...

Remember to apply the highlight only to the tops of the folds in these tight spots.

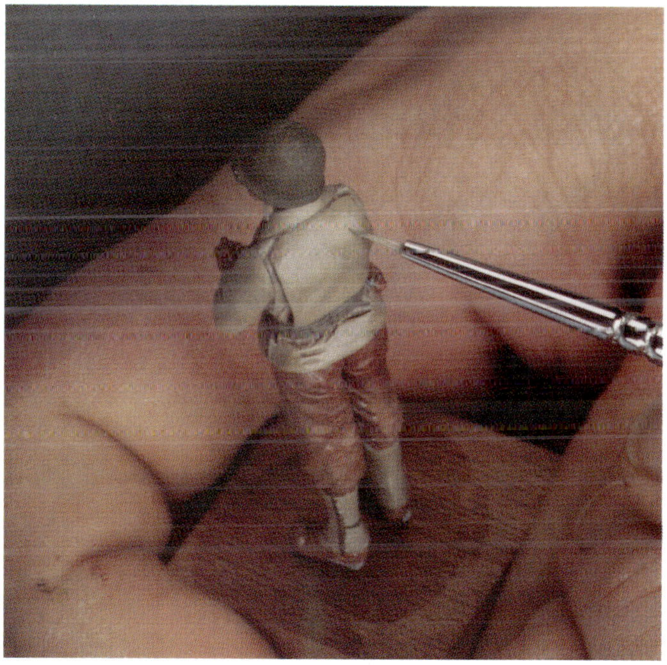

...for this result.

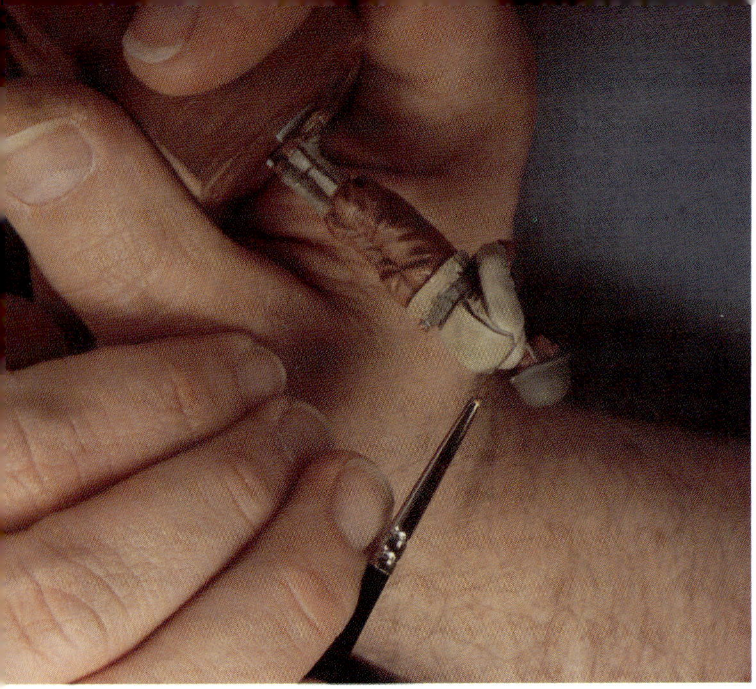

I realized that I had overblended behind the collar. I am going back in with my shadow color to correct my mistake.

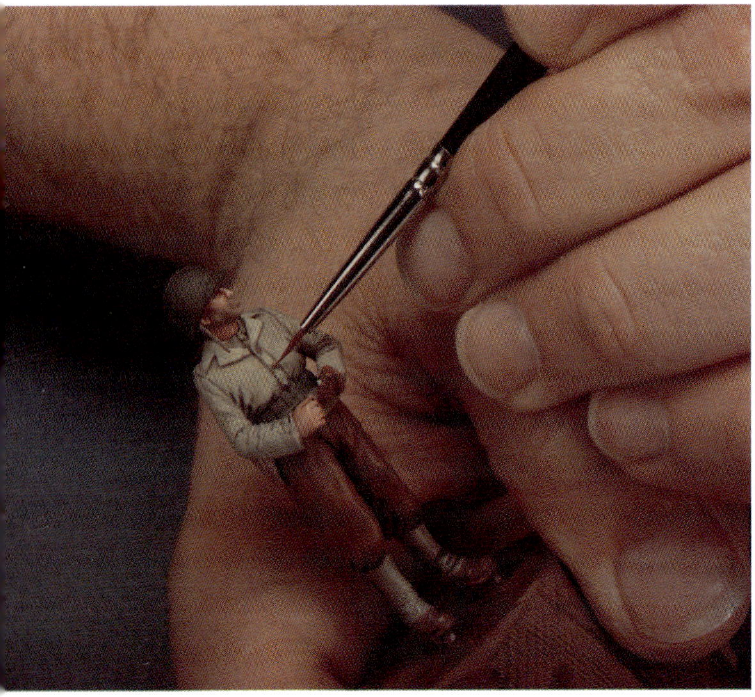

Use dark brown (such as Burnt Sienna) to paint the buttons.

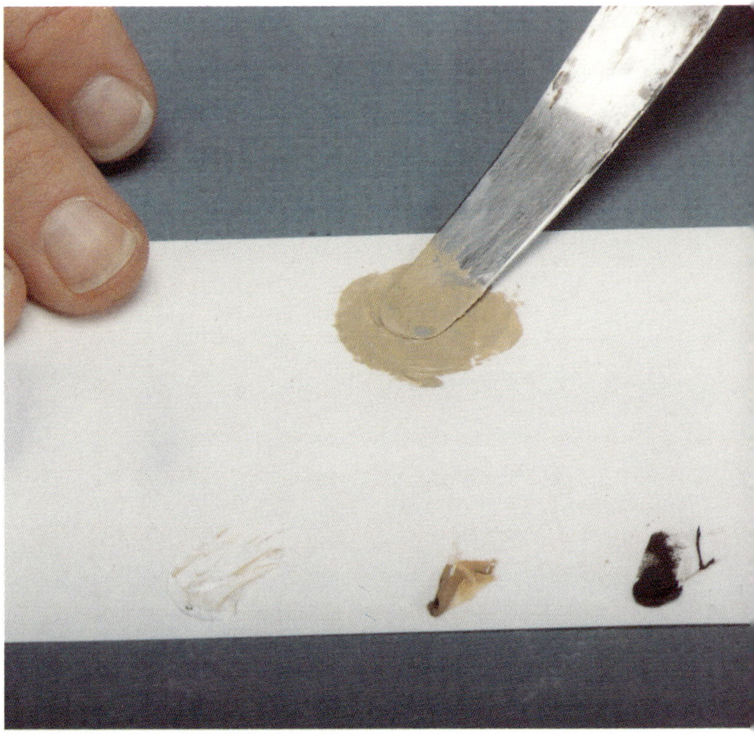

For the canvas leggings, I use the same combination of colors that I used for the jacket except that I add slightly more Yellow Ochre. We will add the same colors to create a highlight and shadow color that we used for the jacket but because our middle color is slightly different, the leggings will also have a slightly different hue.

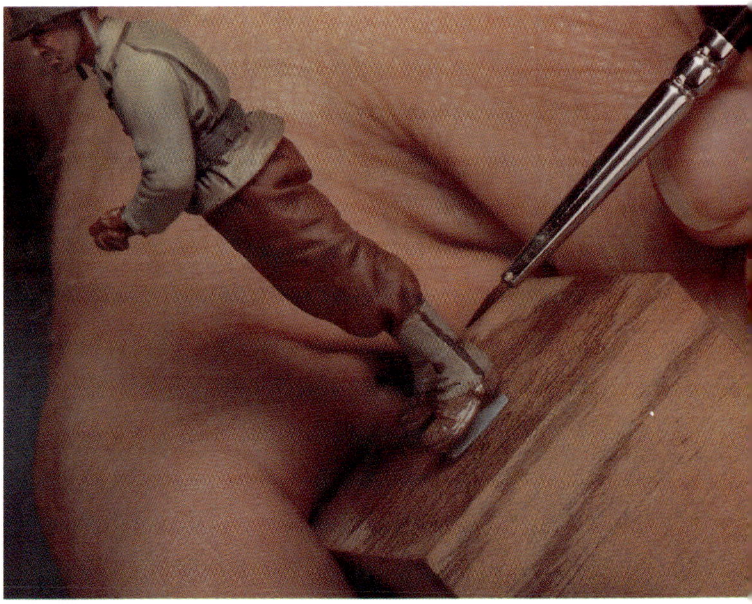

Again, locate the recessed areas and folds on the leggings and apply the shadow color.

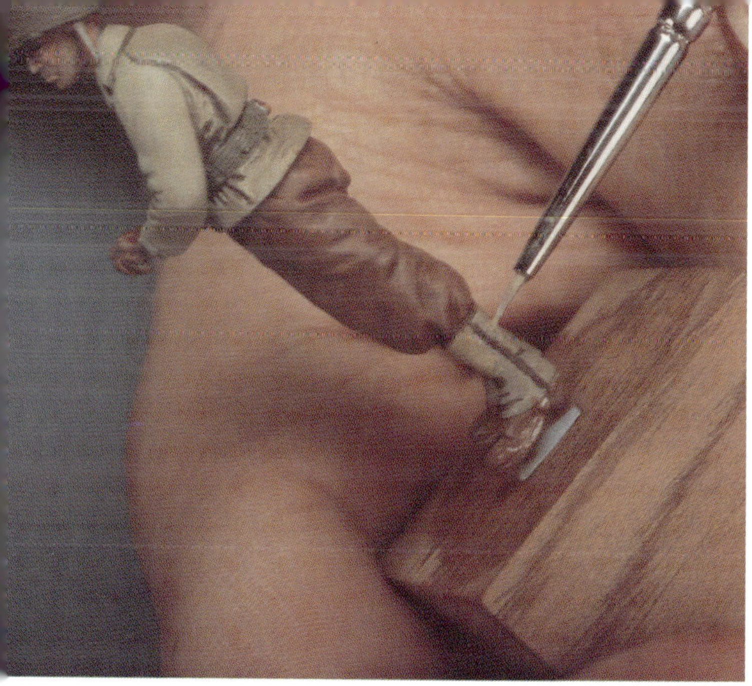

Next apply the middle color, bringing it up next to the shadow color.

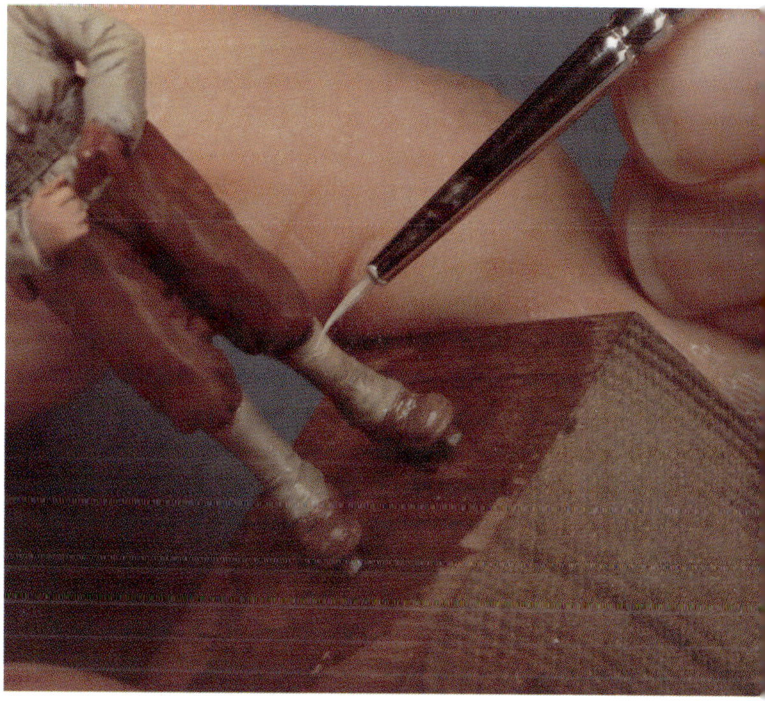

Apply the highlight color to the raised areas.

Blend and soften these two colors.

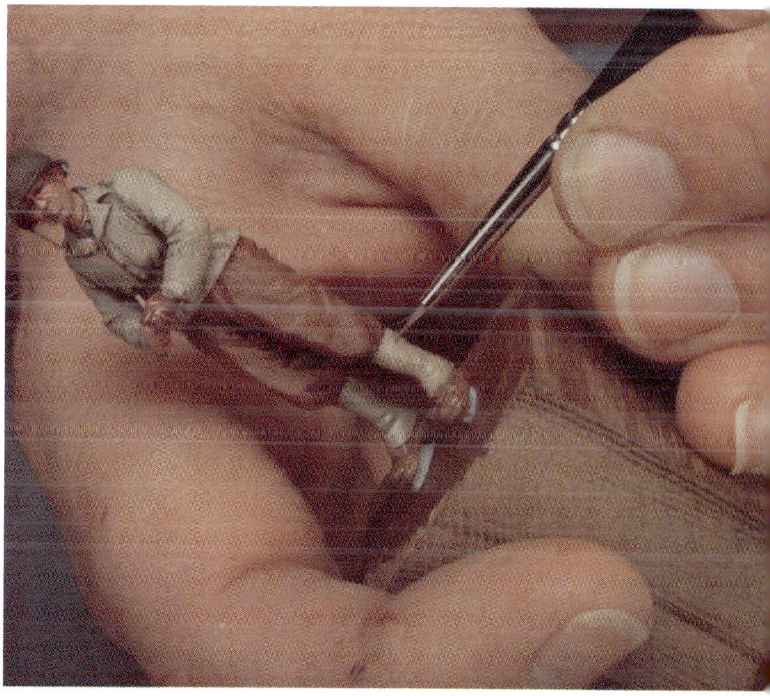

Blend.

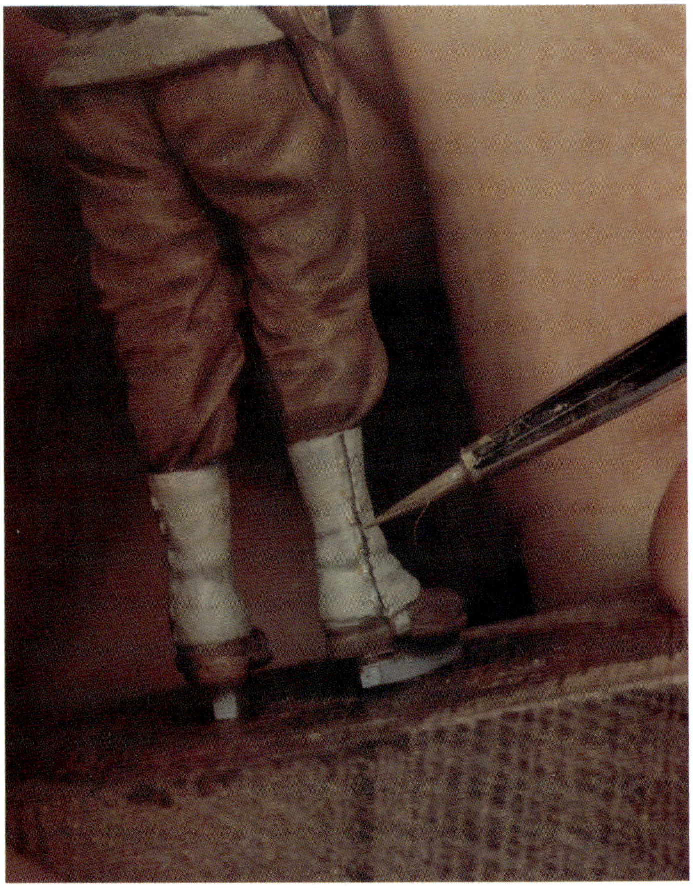

Paint the small studs on the sides of the leggings a golden color. I use Yellow Ochre mixed with Gold hobby paint for this purpose.

The blending is complete.

Also paint the buckle for the legging strap that passes underneath the boot.

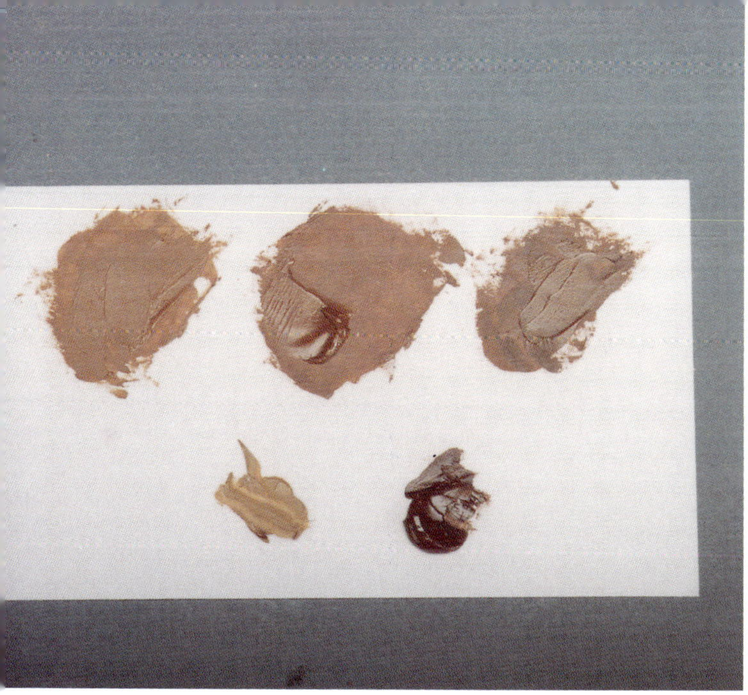

The pants are painted with a mix of Burnt Sienna and Yellow Ochre. Here is the three color mix, creating the highlight and shadow color for the wool trousers.

Apply the shadow color to the recessed areas of the figure.

The shadow color is applied to the back of the figure. Continue on around to the front.

Don't forget to put a line around the top of the legging and the bottom of the jacket.

The applied shadows.

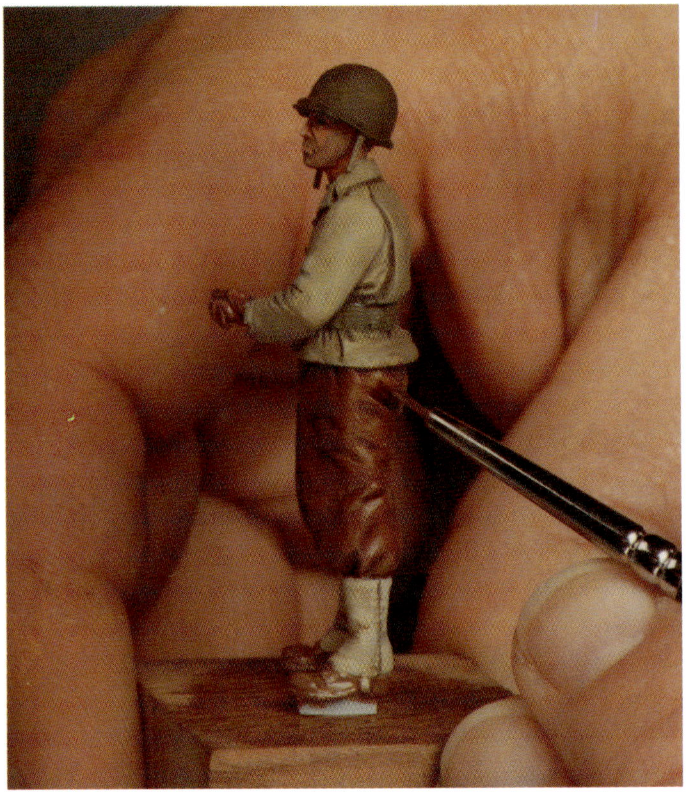

Blend these colors and soften the demarcation line between the middle and shadow colors.

It is time to apply the middle color.

The blended shadow and middle color.

Apply the highlight color to the tops of the folds and any other raised areas.

The pants are completed.

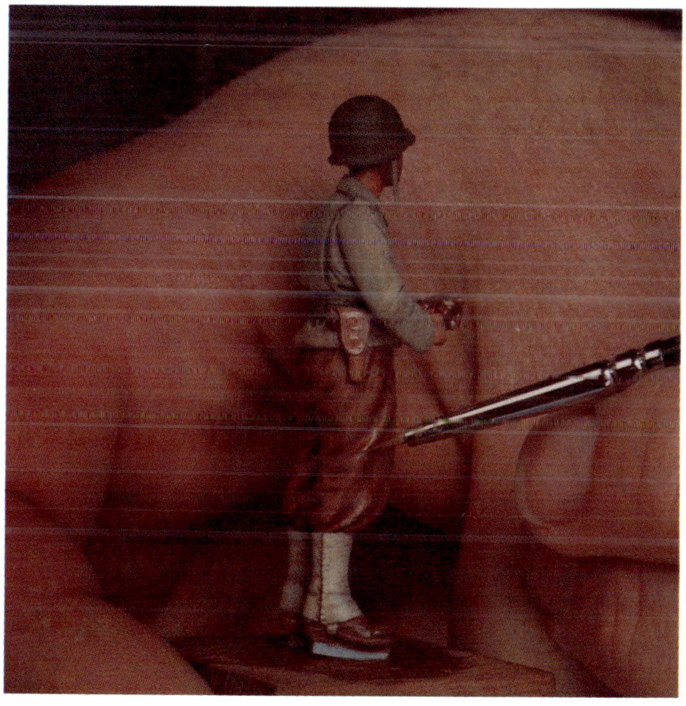

Gently soften these highlights, using a dabbing motion.

A small portion of the shirt and tie are visible on this figure. I mix a variation of the jacket color to paint the tan shirt and tie. The colors I use are Raw Umber, a small amount of Sap Green, Yellow Ochre, and White.

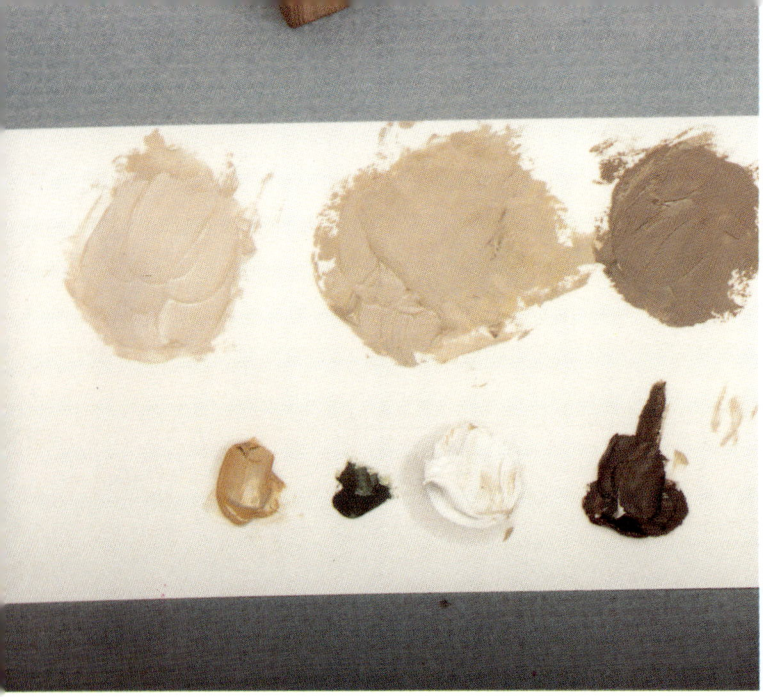

Add a small amount of White to the middle color to create the highlight, and a small amount of Raw Umber to create a shadow color.

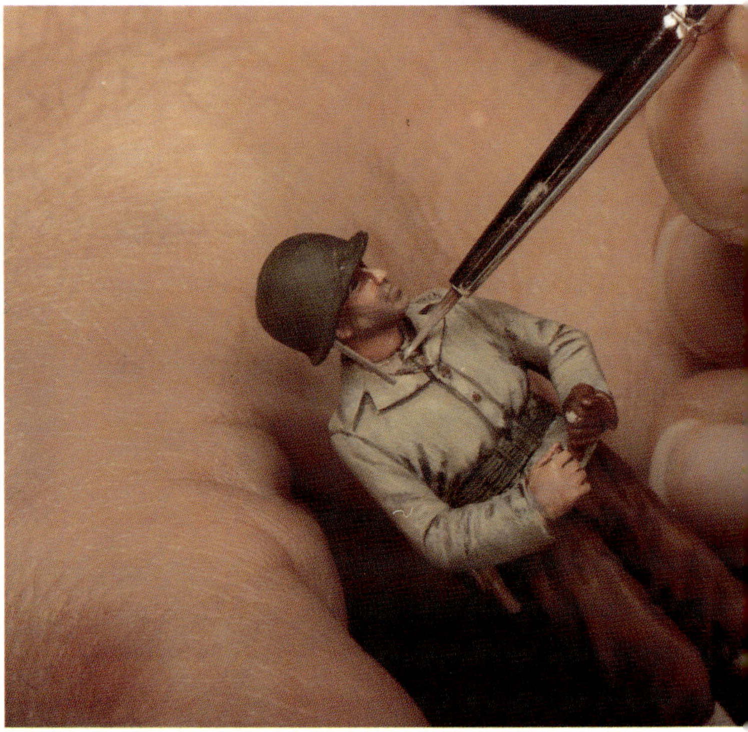

Next apply the middle color.

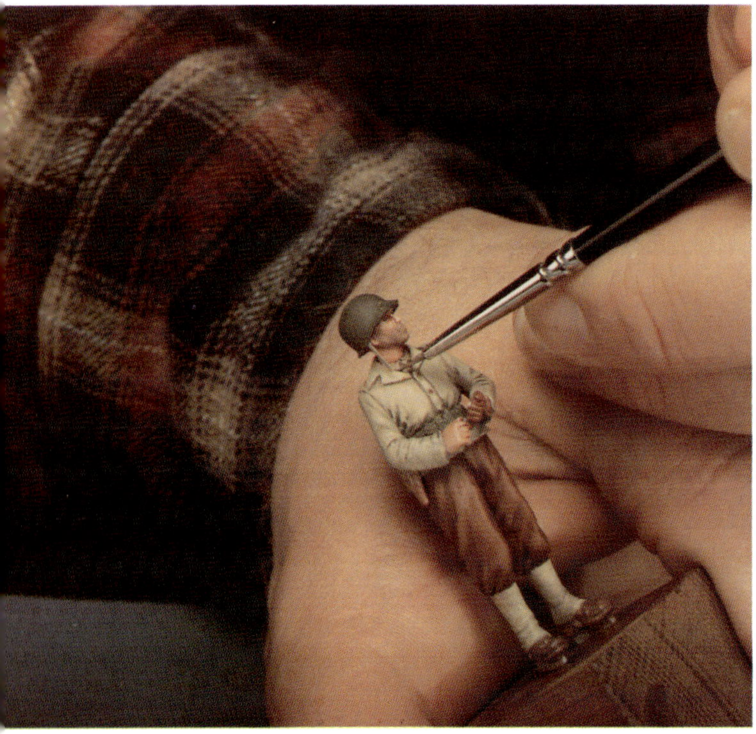

Carefully apply the shadow color where the jacket meets the shirt and where the tie meets the shirt. The shadow color on either side of the tie will be nothing more than just a short, narrow line of color as this is such a small area to work in.

Finally, apply a small dot of highlight color to the knot of the tie and on either side of the tie on the collar.

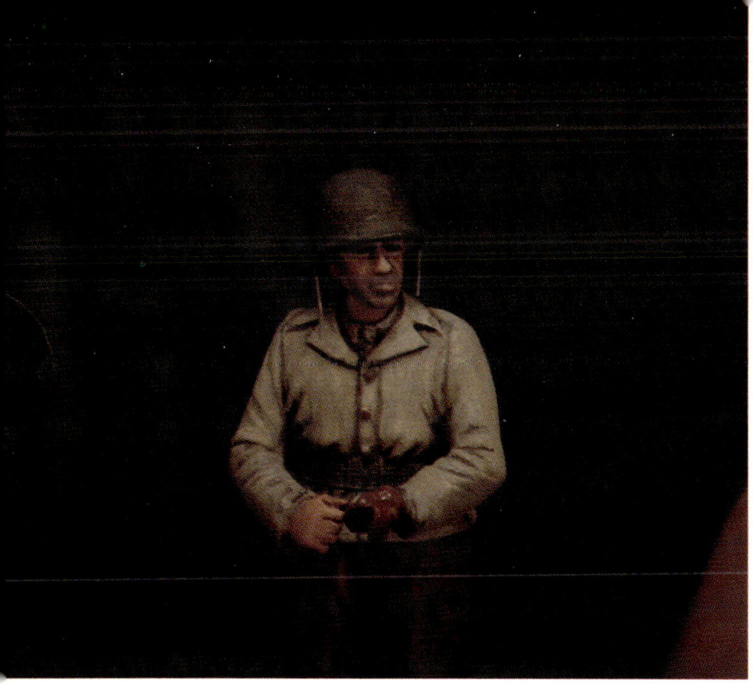

The completed shirt and tie. Be aware that when working in such tight quarters, the highlight color is often a mere dot of color. These small dots of color will make this detail pop out.

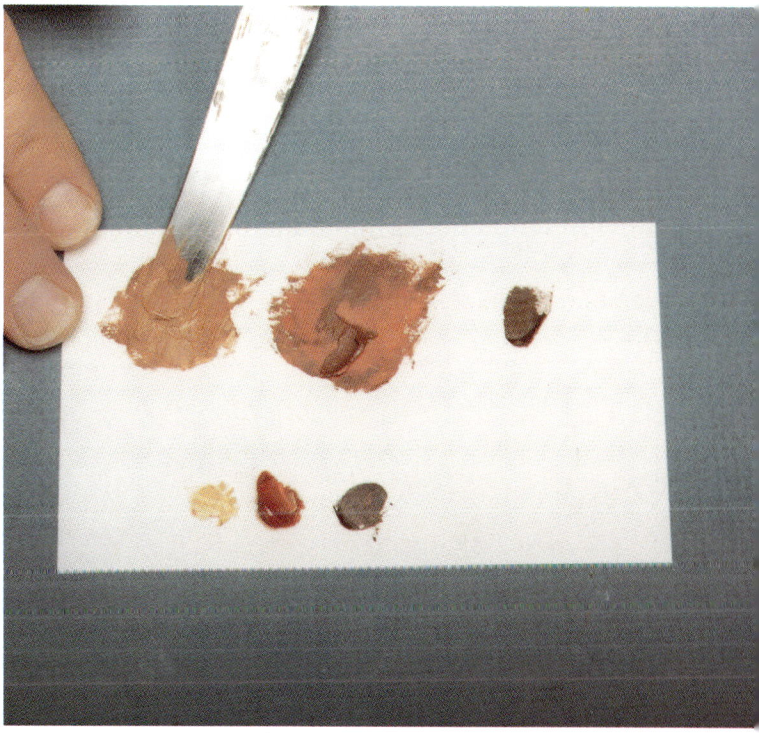

For the shadow color I am using Burnt Sienna straight out of the tube, and for the highlight color I have mixed additional yellow with my middle color.

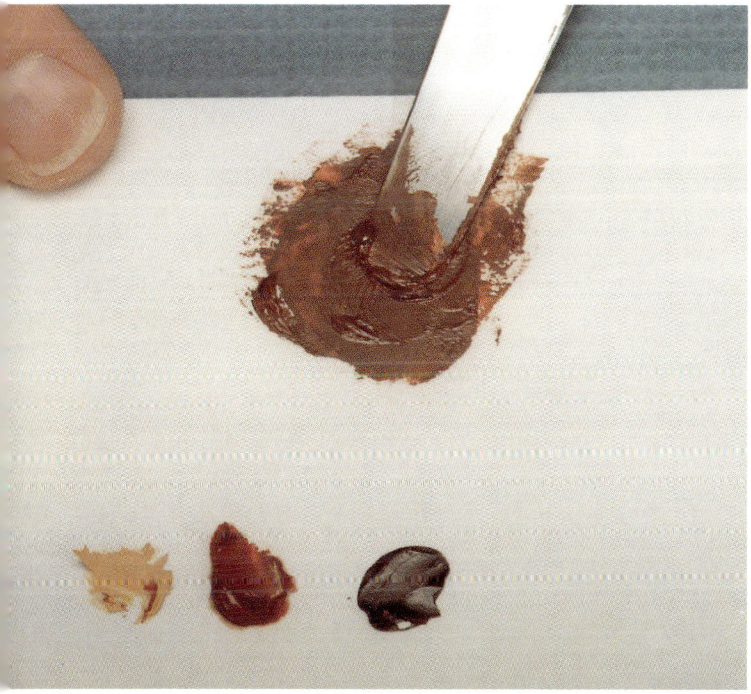

For this figure's gloves, I mixed Cadmium Red, Naples Yellow, and Burnt Sienna to create my middle color.

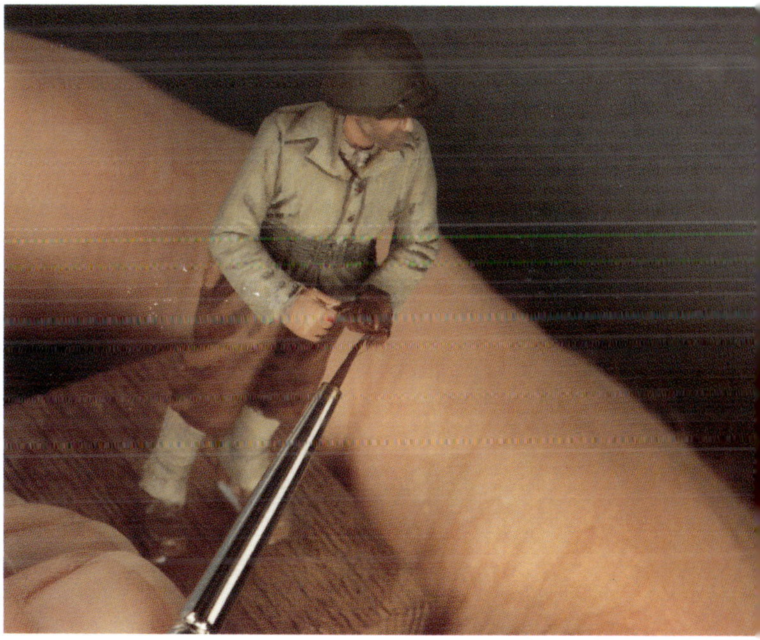

Apply the shadow color using the same process as the shadow color for the hand. Find the recessed areas such as between the fingers and outline where the glove meets the jacket cuff.

Next apply the middle color to the rest of the gloves.

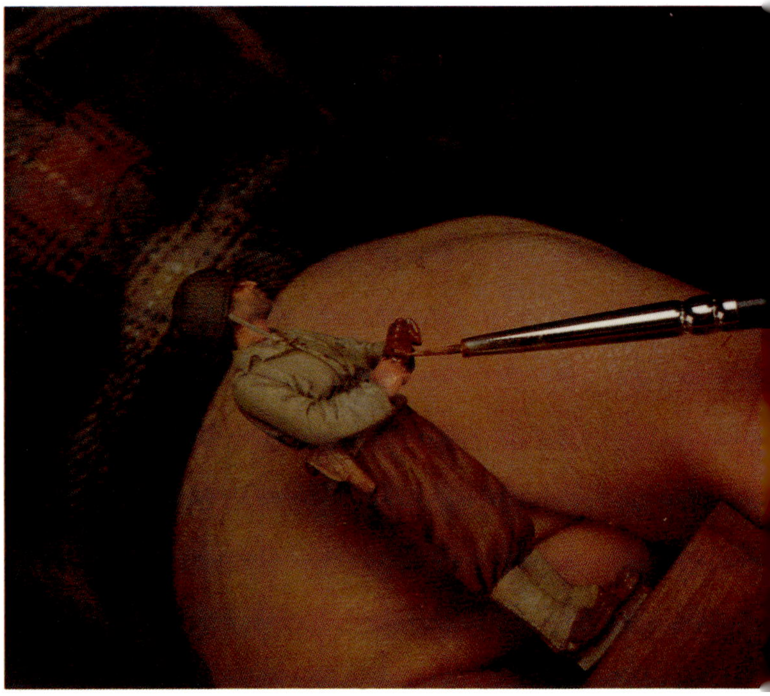

Be careful not to over blend. As with the shirt and tie, you are dealing with a very small area.

Apply the highlight color to the raised ridges on the gloves.

The completed gloves.

Equipment and Accessories

We are now ready to paint the equipment and accessories every soldier carries.

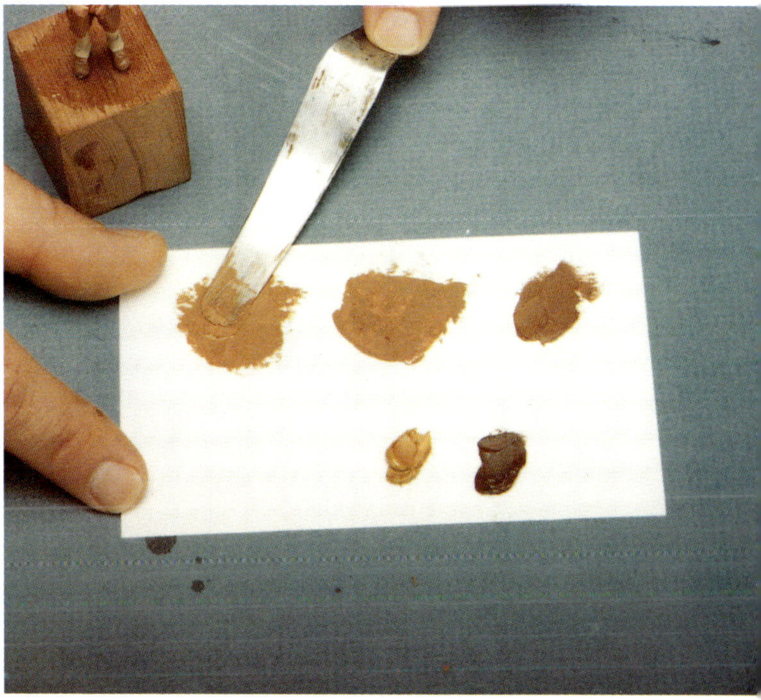

Create a highlight color by adding additional Yellow Ochre and a shadow color with the addition of Burnt Sienna.

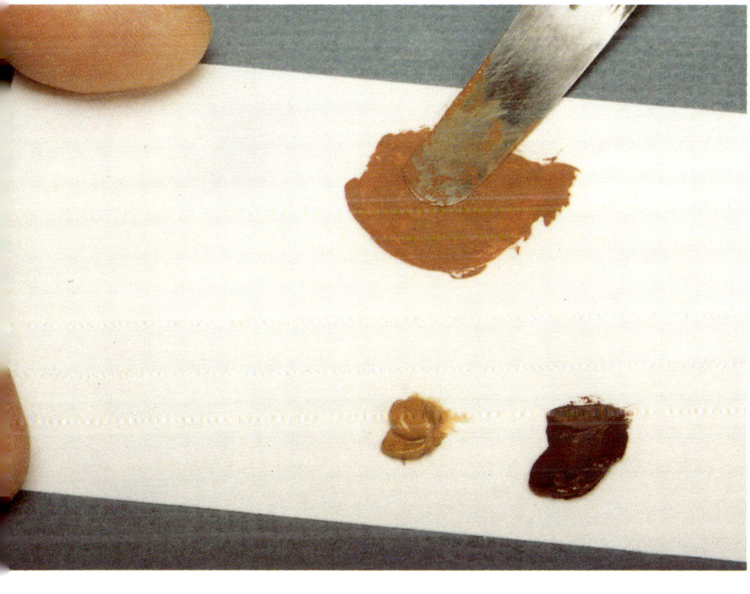

Using Burnt Sienna and Yellow Ochre, I create a light brown color to be used on the figure's boots. This middle color will be much lighter than the color used for the woolen pants even though the same two oil colors have been used in both.

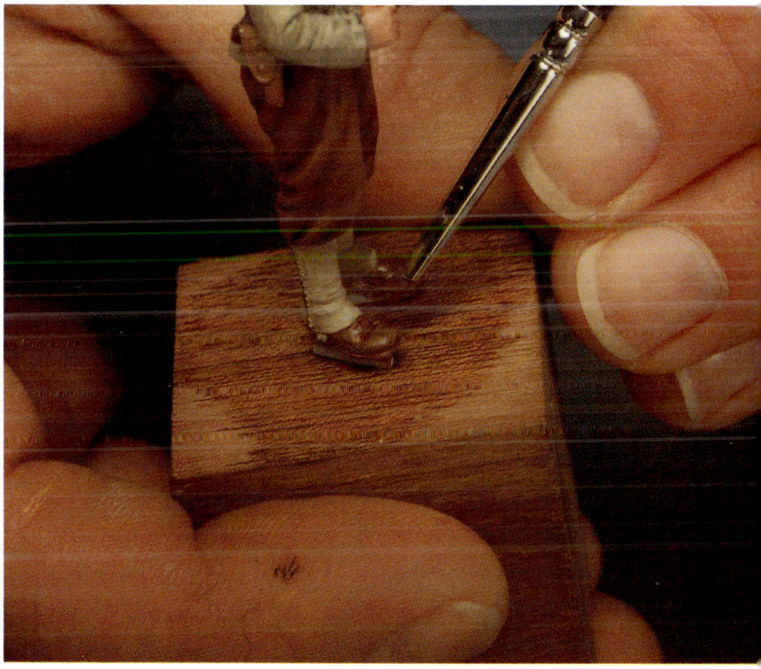

Apply the shadow color to the recessed areas of the folds and seams in the boots.

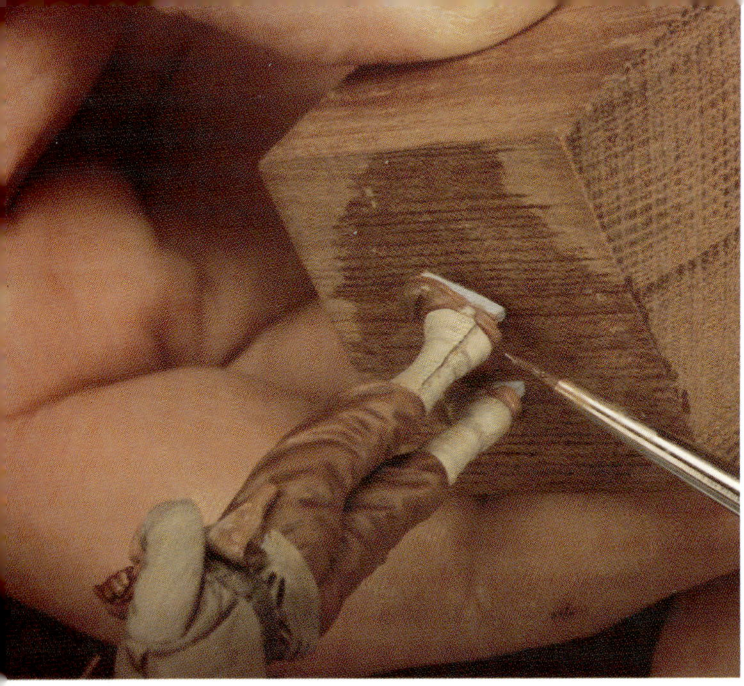

Don't forget to paint the line where the sole meets the shoe's leather upper and where the leggings meet the shoe.

Apply the middle color to the rest of each boot.

The shadow colors applied.

Gently blend using a controlled dabbing motion.

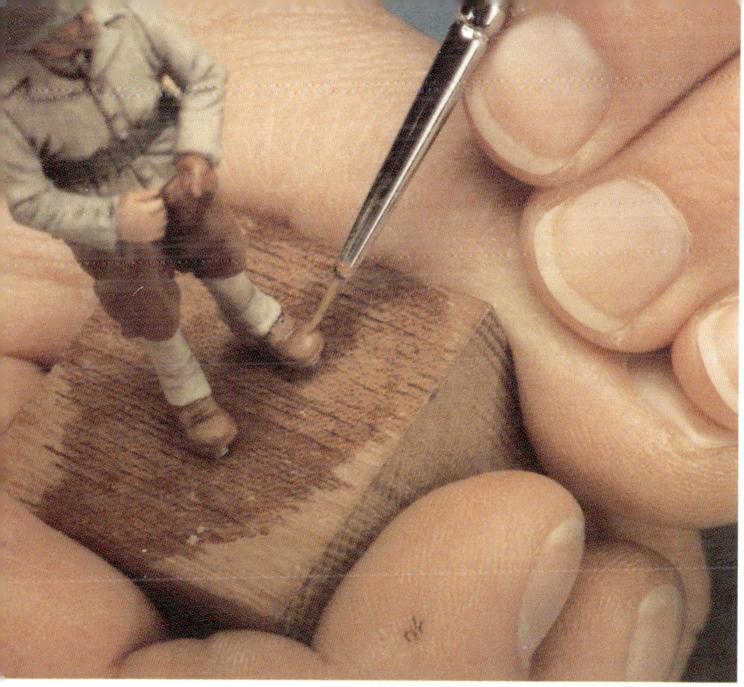

Apply the highlight color to the toes …

Soften the highlights on the toes.

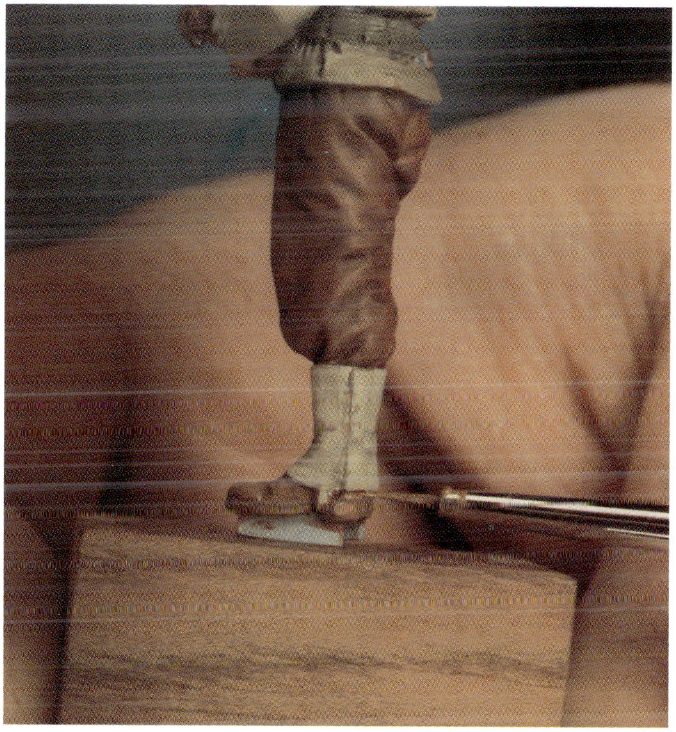

…and a thin line below the leggings and above the heel of the boot.

The finished boots.

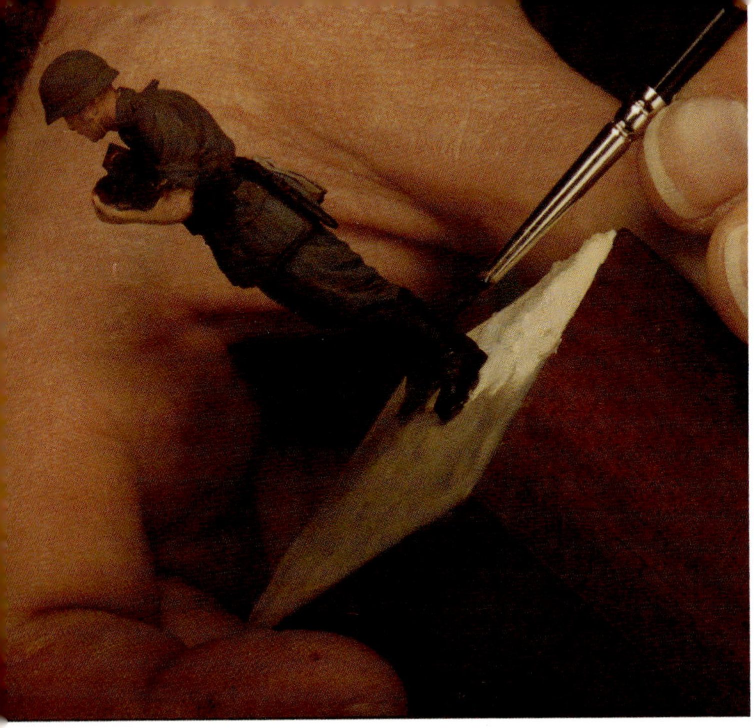

In the case of black leather boots, we will paint the recessed areas with straight Ivory Black as in the case of this German's boots.

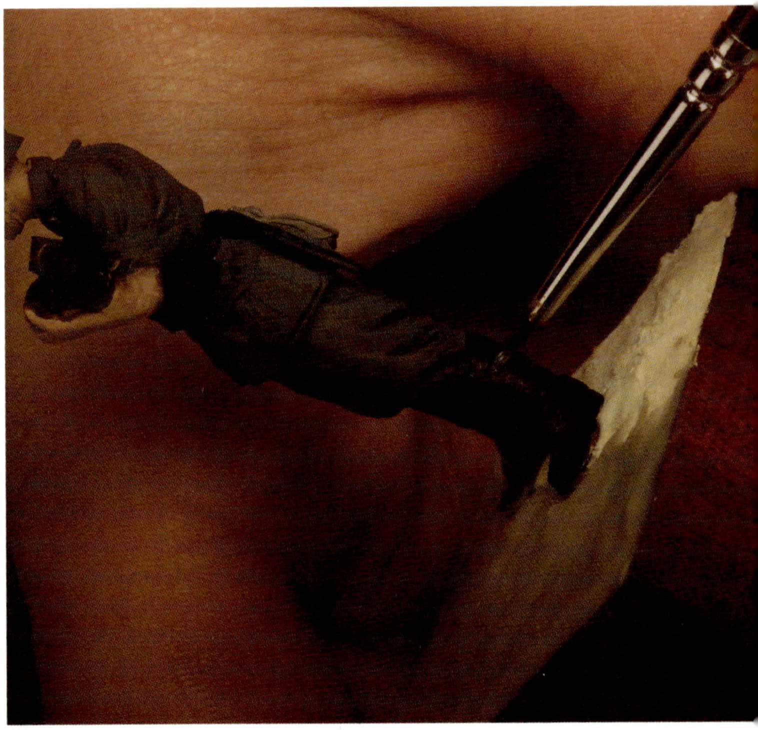

Apply the middle black color.

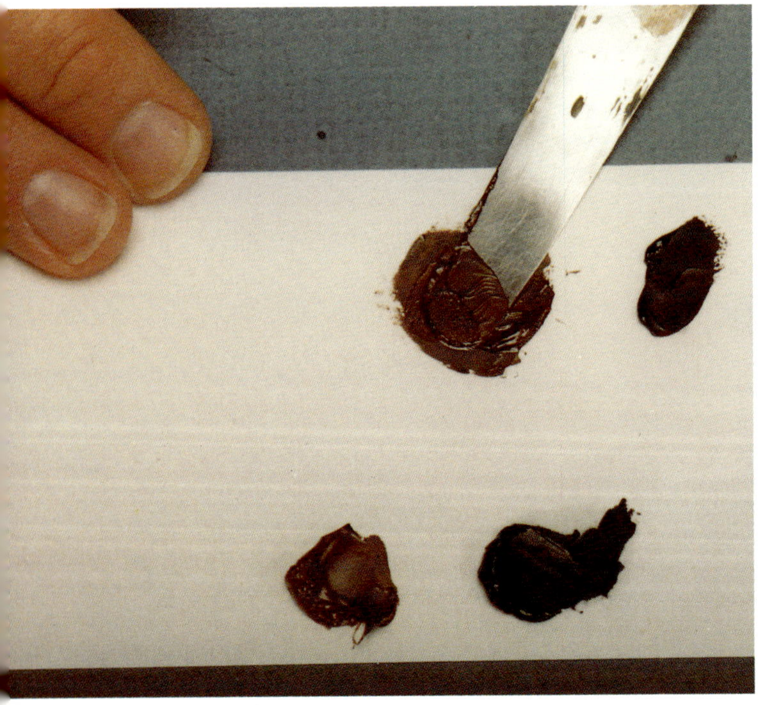

For a middle color mix Burnt Sienna and Black together. Be mindful that you want to keep this color very dark.

For a highlight color add additional Burnt Sienna.

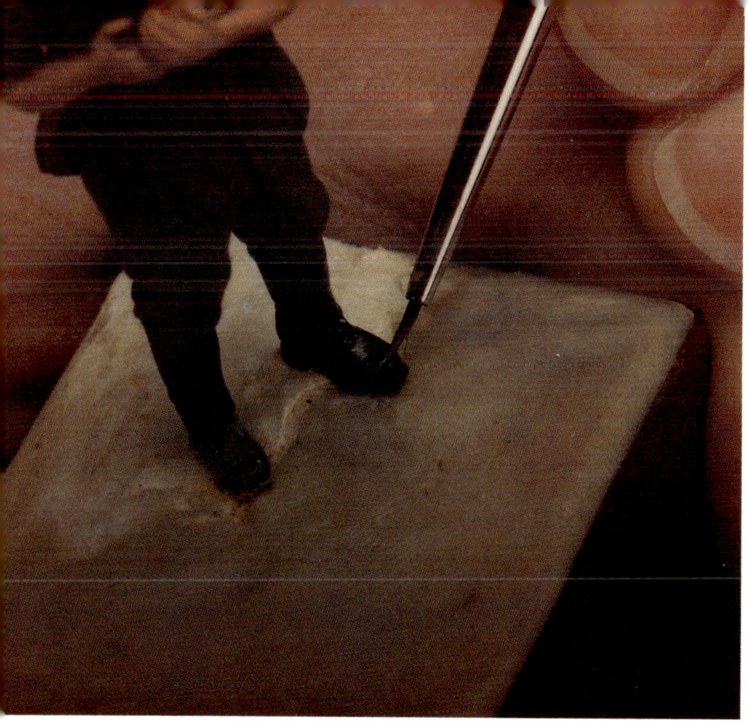

Apply this to the toes and any areas that would pick up highlights.

Pay special attention to the toe and the heel areas of the boots.

If you wish to show extreme wear and tear and heavy use on black leather, mix a dark gray color and apply it in the same manner as the soiled color to the uniform.

The completed boots.

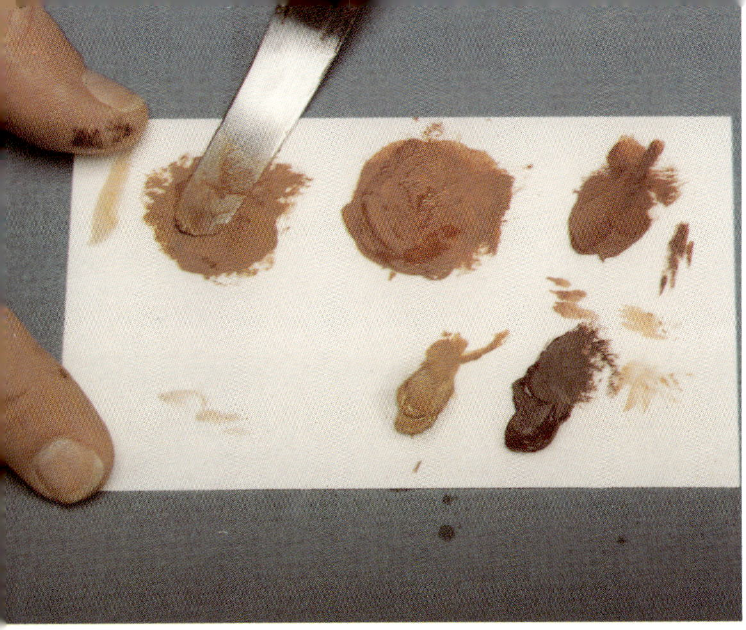

For the figure's brown leather pistol holster, I mixed up a slight variation of the brown boot color. Leather equipment will vary in color from item to item, therefore you have a wide variety of brown shades from which to use. The middle brown is a mix of Burnt Sienna and Yellow Ochre.

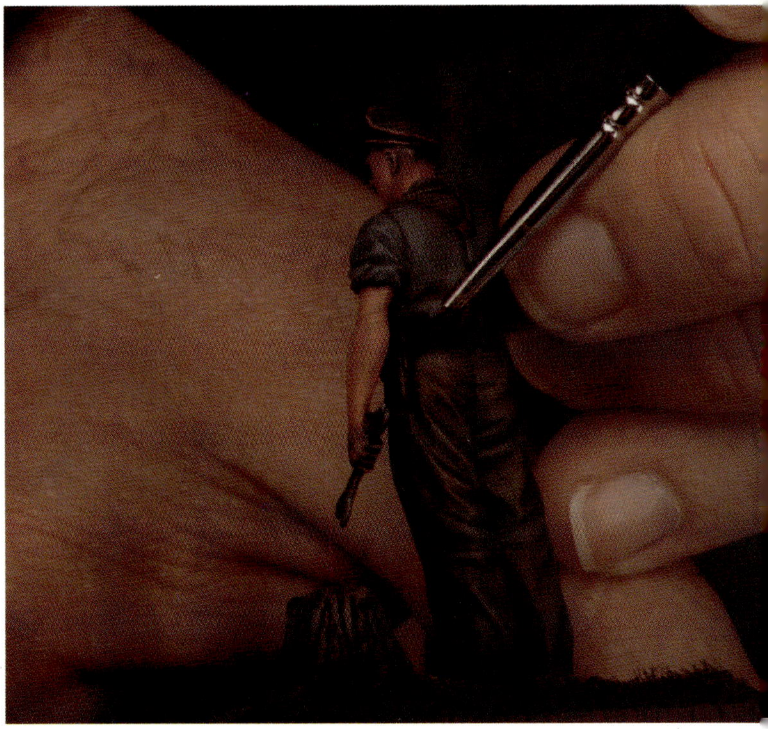

For black leather holsters I use the same colors and techniques as when painting black boots.

I have painted the holster using the same techniques used on the boots, applying the shadow underneath the flap and around the raised areas followed by the middle color and then highlighted to complete the holster.

For the American helmet middle color, I mix Burnt Umber, Sap Green, and White together.

Add Burnt Umber to the middle color to create a shadow color and additional White to the middle color to create a highlight.

Outline the chin strap on the helmet.

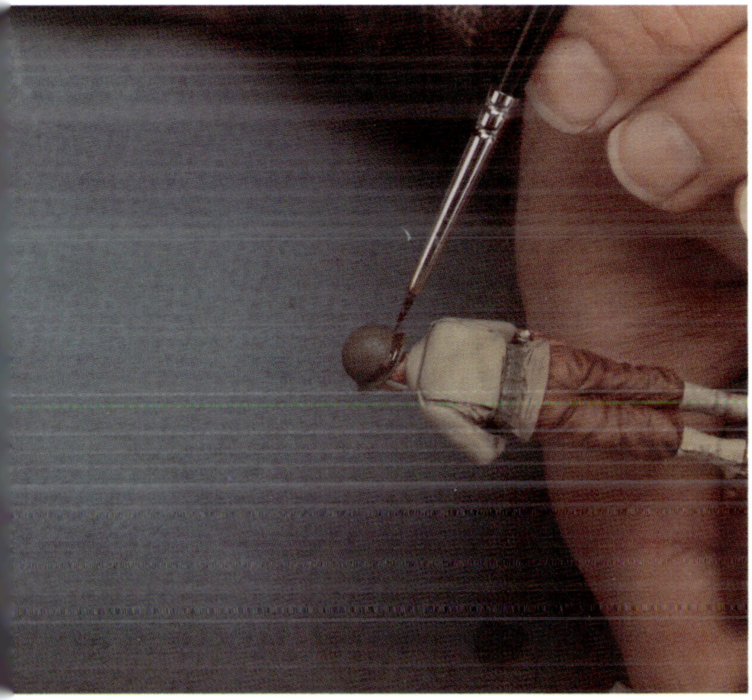

Apply the shadow color in a band along the lower third of the helmet. Be careful not to apply your shadow color on the rolled edge of the helmet.

Apply the middle color to the rest of the helmet and soften the demarcation line between the middle and shadow color.

After blending the middle and shadow colors, add the highlight color to the top of the helmet.

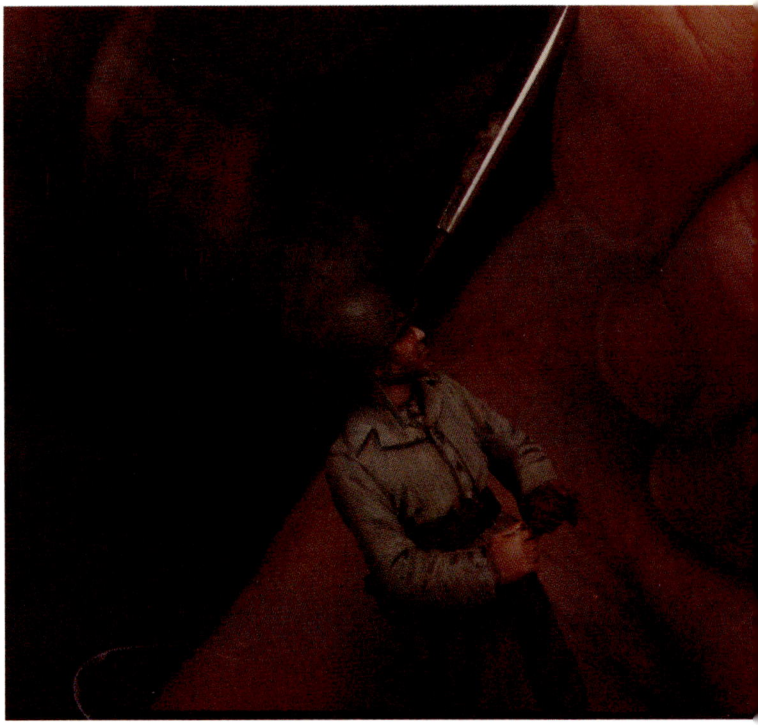

After painting the helmet's chin strap a light greenish-beige color, paint the brown leather strap that crosses the front of the helmet with a reddish-brown. You may use hobby paint for both.

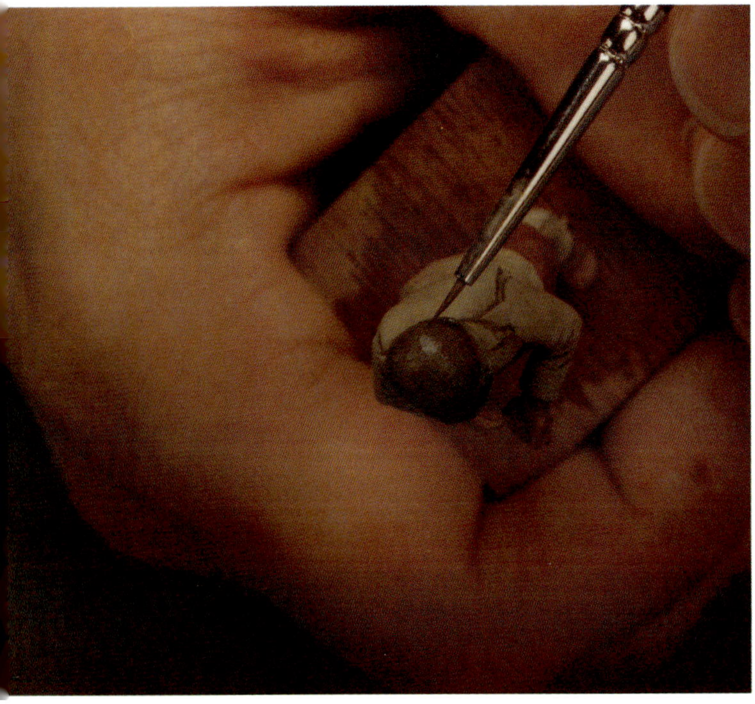

Work the highlight color from the top toward the sides of the helmet. Be careful not to work the color too far down or you will lose all of the contrast you have worked so hard to create.

When painting helmets that have helmet nets on them, such as our walking G.I., lighten your helmet highlight color. After loading some of the color onto a brush, wipe off the excess on a piece of paper. This will leave very little paint on your brush.

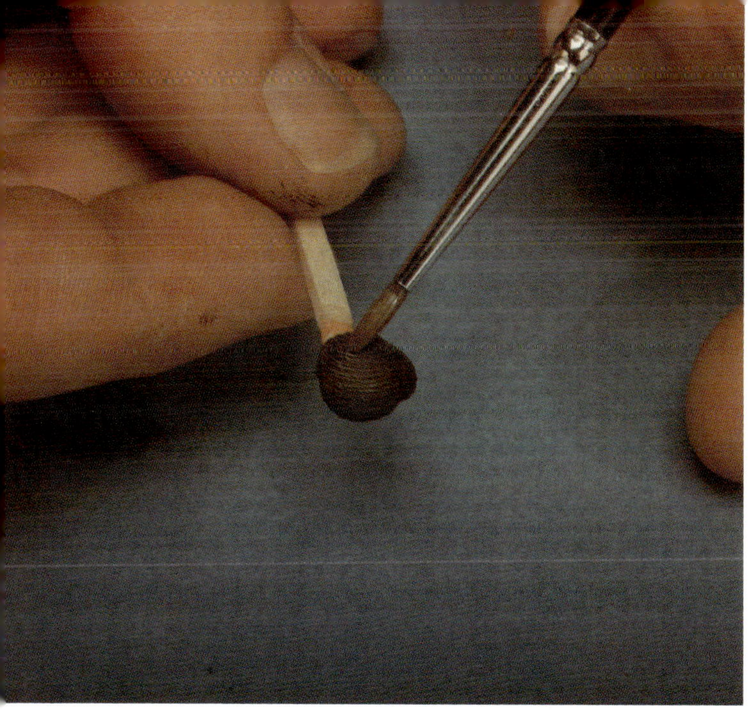

Gently drag the brush across the surface of the netting. The raised areas of the net will pick up slight amounts of the almost dried paint off of the brush. This technique is called dry brushing and will be used when painting many of the accessories on the figure.

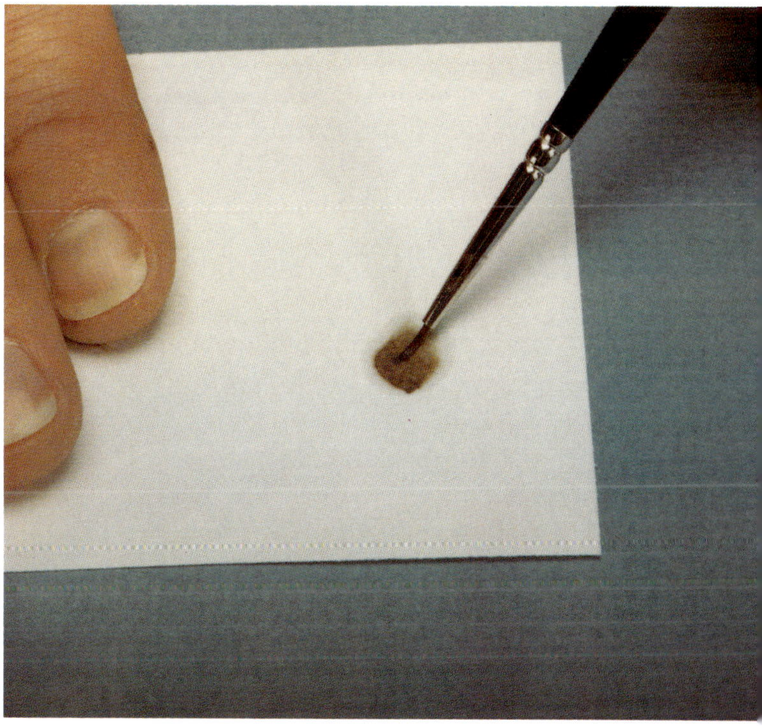

To easily pick out the minute detail on this G.I.'s belt, thin down Raw Umber with turpentine to create a "wash."

The finished G.I. with the completed helmet.

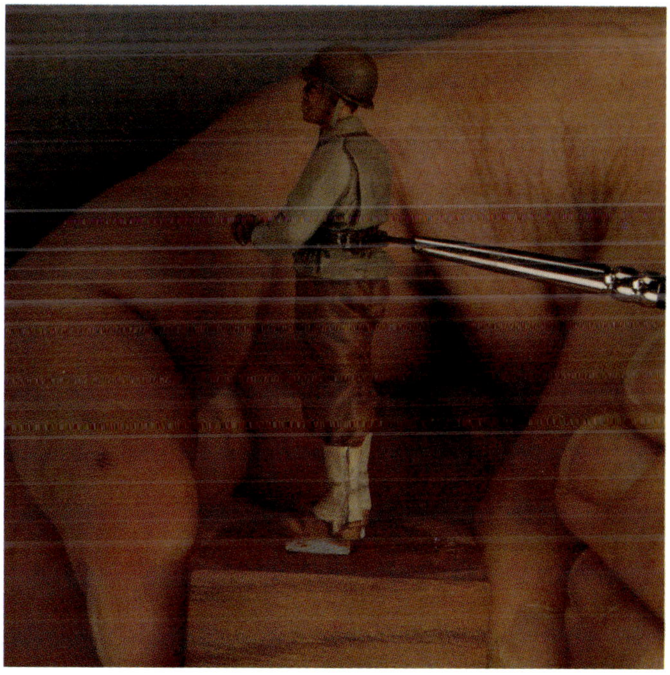

Carefully apply a small amount of this wash to the undercoated belt and allow it to dry. This will act as our shadow color.

Using the dry brush method, apply a medium green color. The color that you use for the web belts can range from pale olive to beige. Try to dry brush from top to bottom so that only the raised ridges pick up the color leaving your dark brown wash in the grooves.

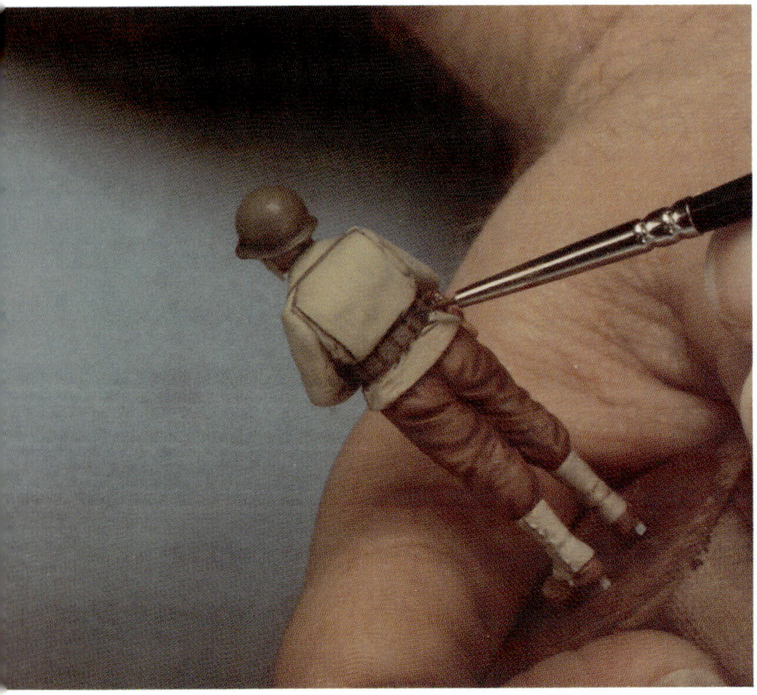

Add a small amount of white to the belt color just used and again using the dry brush method carefully apply it starting along the top of the upper edge of the belt as shown in the photo. The use of a color wash has changed our approach but the three color methodology remains the same.

The same process used on the figure's web belt can also be applied to such things as American canteen covers that have heavy stitching in the center or any other item that has tiny grooves or details.

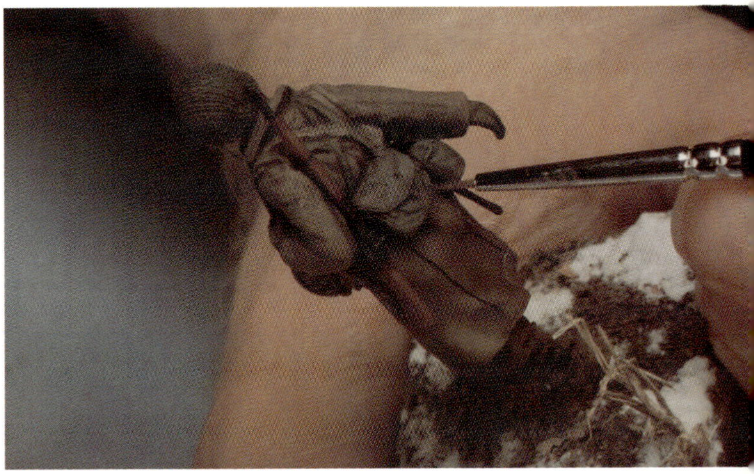

Continue on with the three color process, varying the colors slightly for each item until all of the equipment is painted. This will include backpacks, first aid pouches, or any and all other webbed gear.

The waist belts on these German figures were painted black using the same technique and colors as we used when painting black holsters. This also will apply to the black leather cartridge pouches worn by German infantrymen.

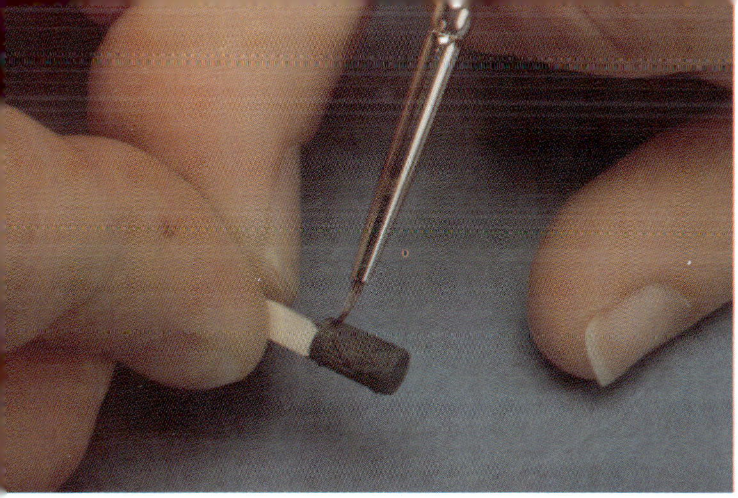

For painted metal items such as this German gas mask container, first undercoat it with the appropriate color and then ...

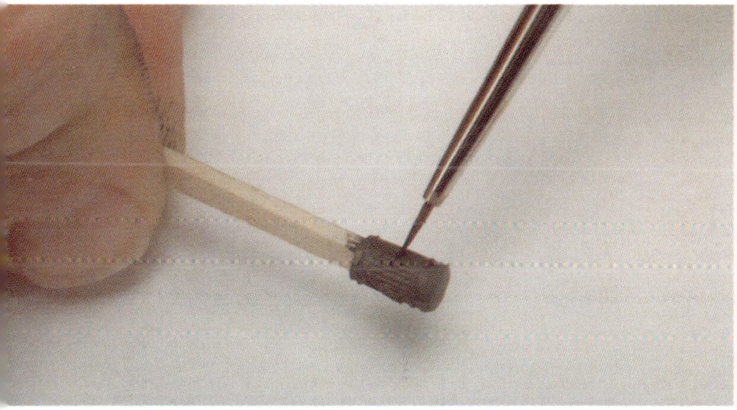

...apply a wash of shadow color and let dry thoroughly.

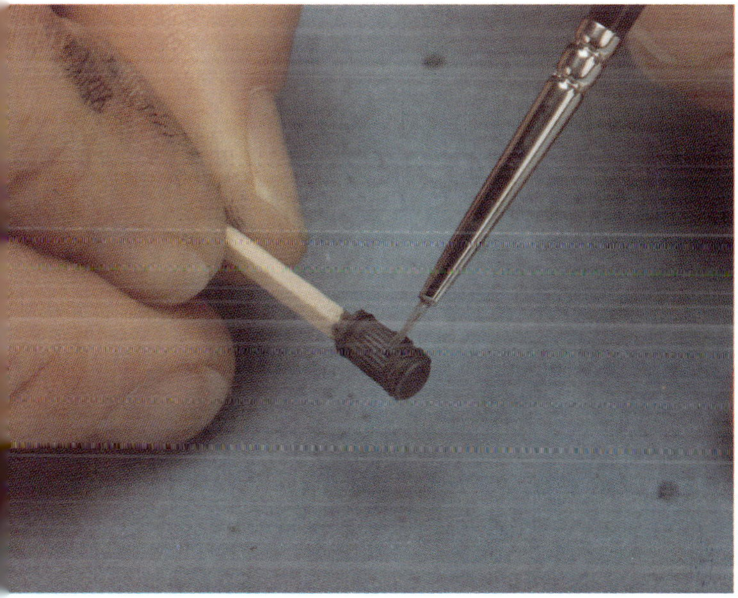

Using the field gray oil paint mixture, dry brush the item.

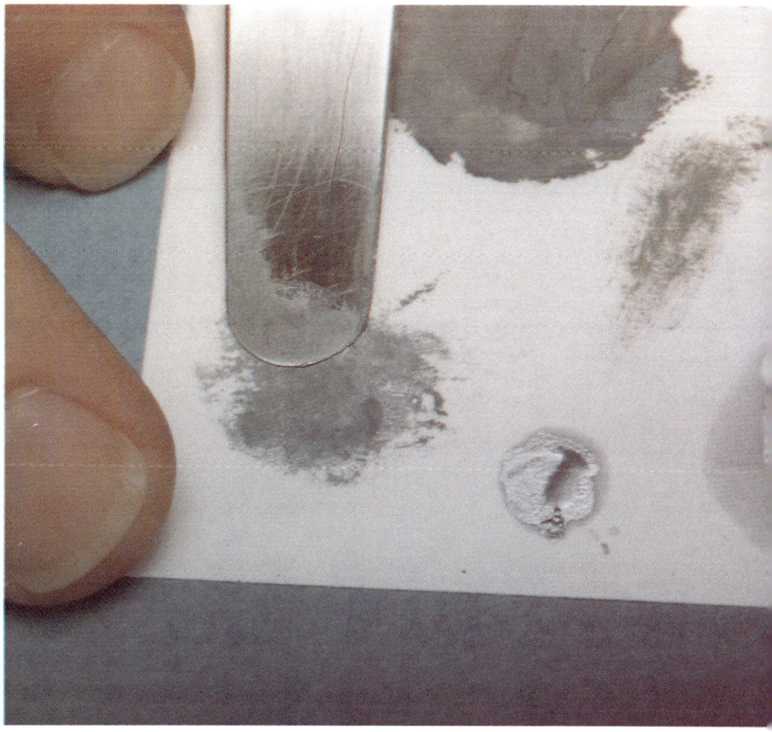

If you wish to show areas where the paint has worn through to the metal underneath, mix a small amount of silver hobby paint with your highlight oil color. Be careful not to add too much silver as you want the effect of the paint slowly wearing through to metal.

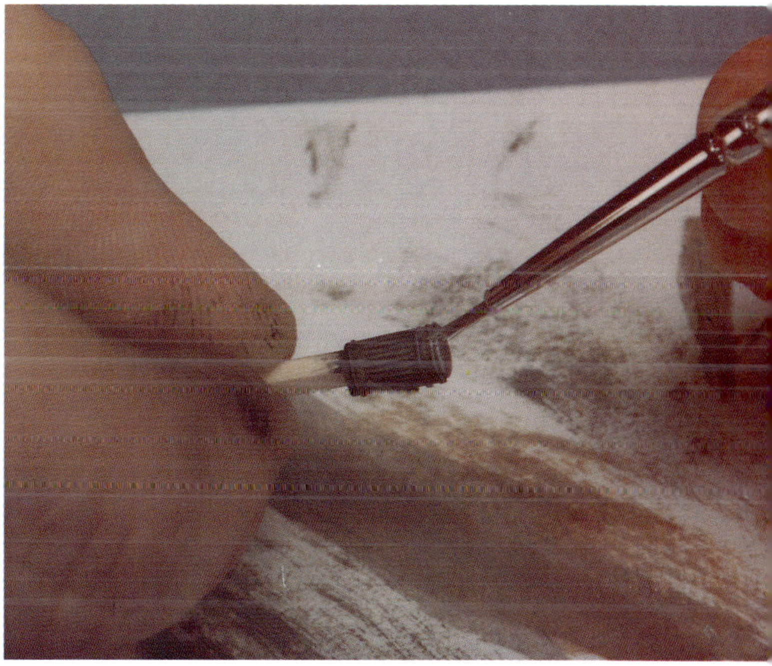

Apply this silvery field gray color to areas that would naturally be worn or rubbed such as the edge of the container and random areas on the body of the item. The more you apply, the more worn the item will appear.

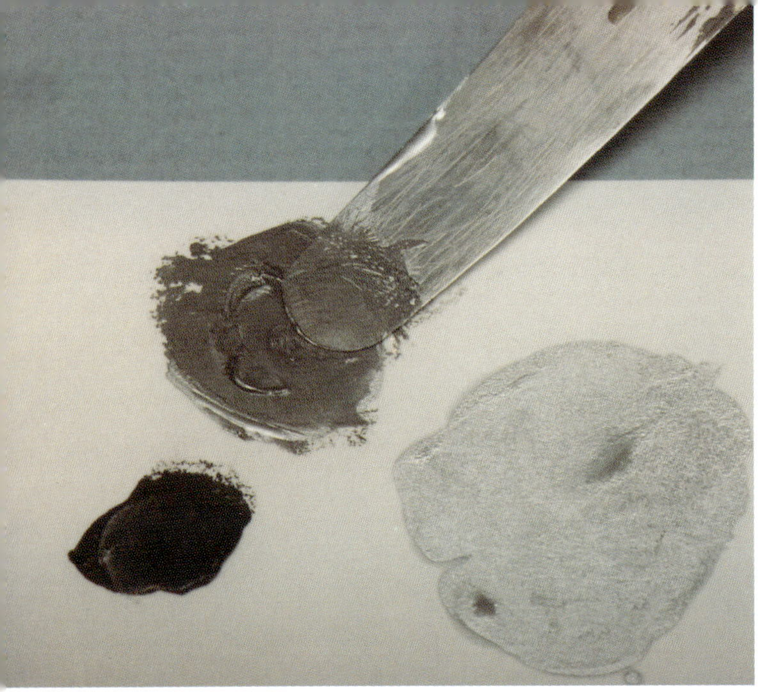

For silver colored metal items, such as German belt buckles, buttons, etc., I mix silver hobby paint and black oil paint to create a dull steel color.

This also is used for metal insignias on the uniform and cap. For silver colored cloth insignias I use the same technique except that I mix silver and white hobby paint together to create a slightly different look.

After painting buckles black I dry brush my dull steel color onto the raised areas.

To paint the white cloth eagle and wreath on this German tanker I carefully dry brush white oil paint on the raised area of the beret. The red center dot of the roundel was painted after that.

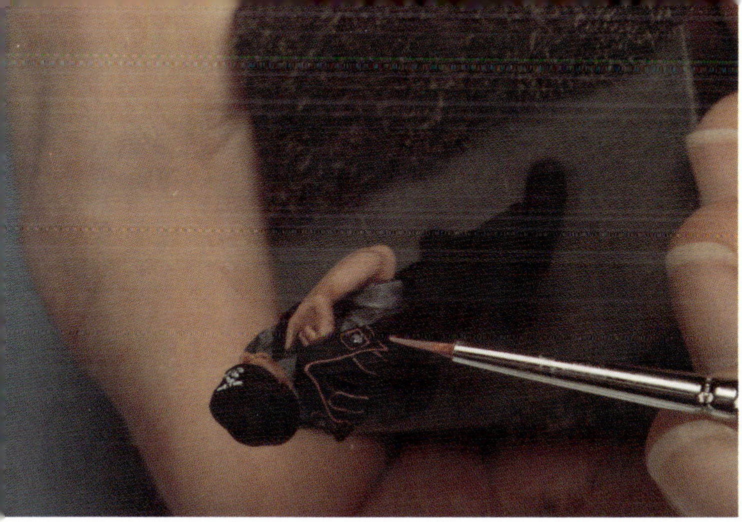

The pink piping on the German tanker's jacket was made by mixing Cadmium Red and Titanium White and then carefully applied to the appropriate areas. For small thin lines such as this you may also use hobby paints as there is very little shading or highlighting that can be done.

Rommel's binoculars were painted black using the three shades of black technique used previously. Oftentimes binoculars were painted tan for desert use, in which case you would use different shades of tan instead of black.

Gold trim is handled in the same manner. When painting gold, such as on this figure of Rommel, I undercoat those areas with dark brown hobby paint and then dry brush gold as we did with the silver colors.

I painted the scarf as though it were a light color using my three color method. After that was completely dried I added thin lines of red and blue to create a plaid pattern. The thin red line around the epaulets on Rommel's coat were added with red hobby paint.

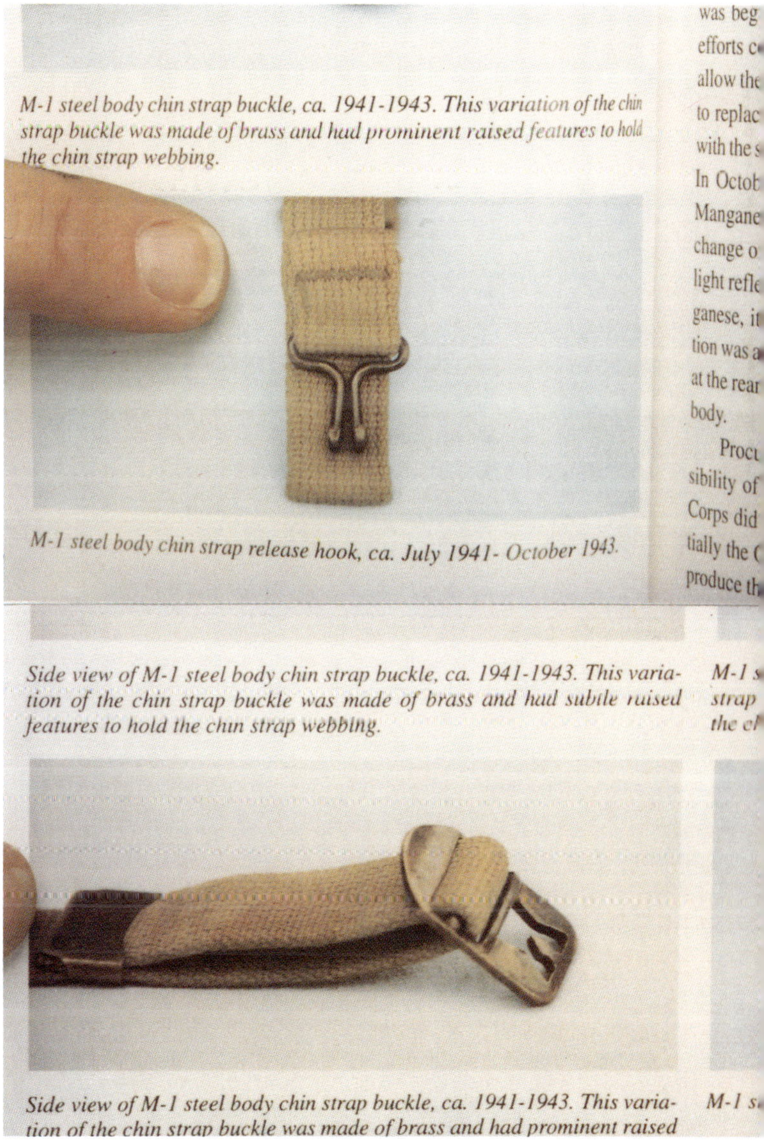

Checking our reference material for our helmet chin straps, we find there are two metal fasteners which must be painted.

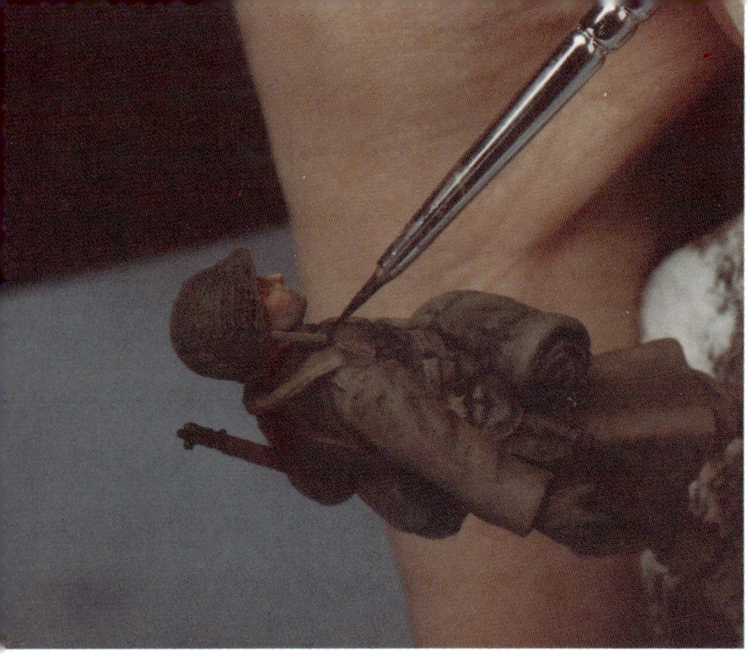

Paint these using Burnt Umber. Keep in mind these fasteners will not appear as much more than small dots on the chin strap.

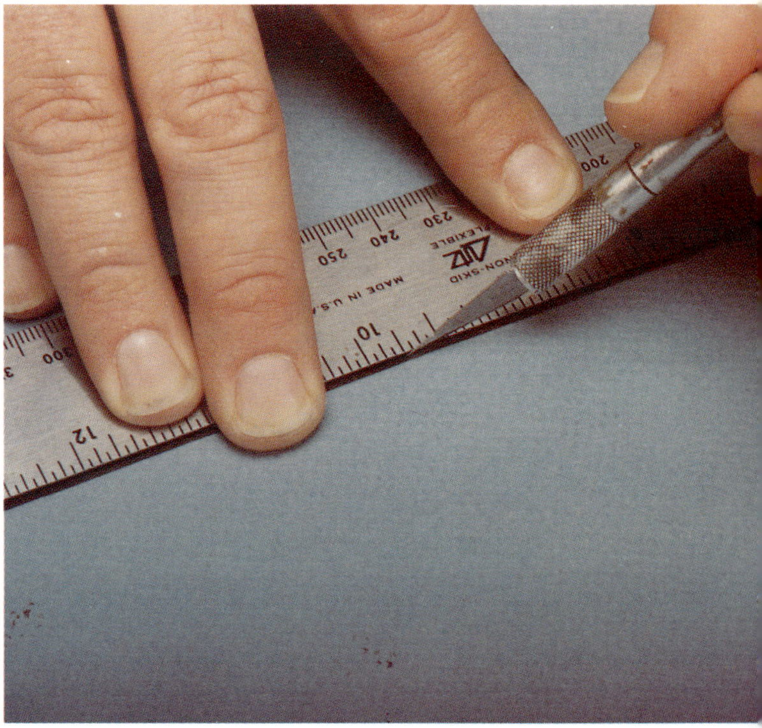

Cut an appropriate width of material.

For helmets that do not have molded on chin straps I like to cut a piece of electrical tape that has had the sticky backing removed by soaking momentarily in turpentine. Wipe off the residue with a rag.

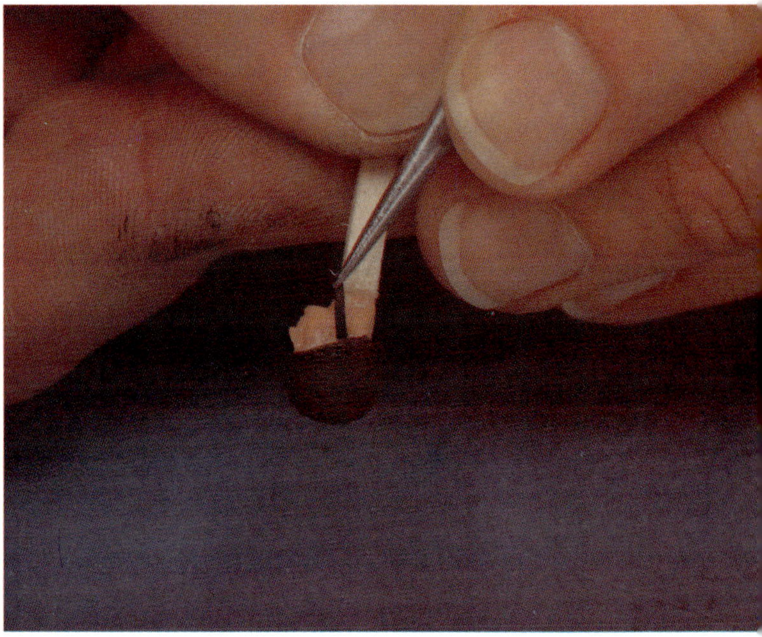

After cutting the strap to the appropriate length, dip it in a drop of cyanoacrylate glue and attach it to the proper location on the helmet. On American helmets, one strap is longer than the other.

Weapons

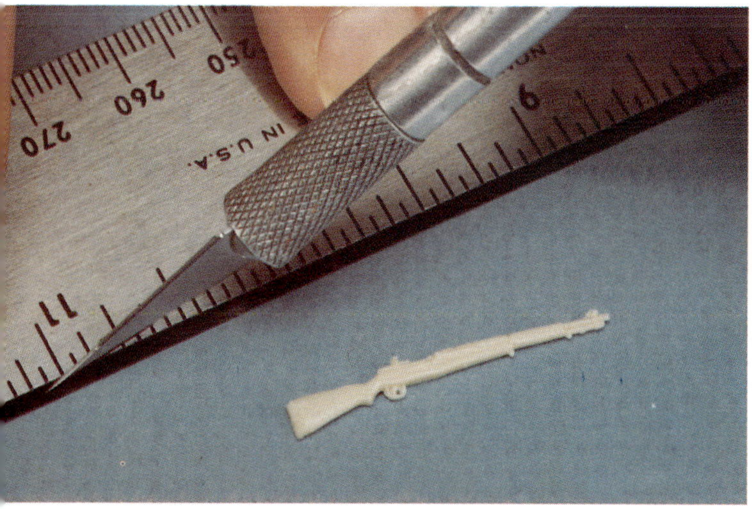

Before painting a weapon, first decide if you would like to add a sling, as in the case of this rifle. Use electrical tape, cleaned of adhesive with turpentine, as strap material. Cut a piece to the correct length. Usually slings are folded over onto themselves, and therefore will need to be cut much longer than the locations of the attachment points would indicate.

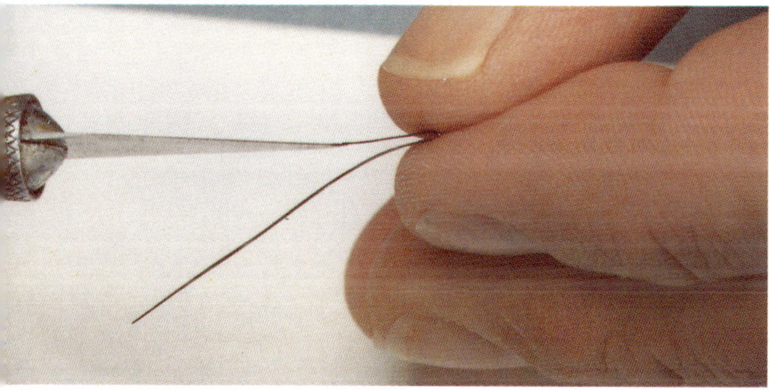

An X-acto blade with a small amount of cyanoacrylate glue on the tip is the perfect applicator when you need to get a small amount of glue on the folded end of your sling.

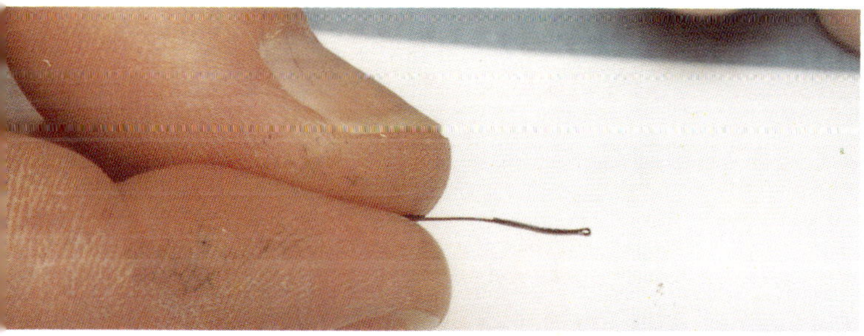

The sling loop has been created. Before repeating this process on the other end of the sling, determine the length needed to reach the second attachment point. The sling could be adjusted to be very taut or very loose.

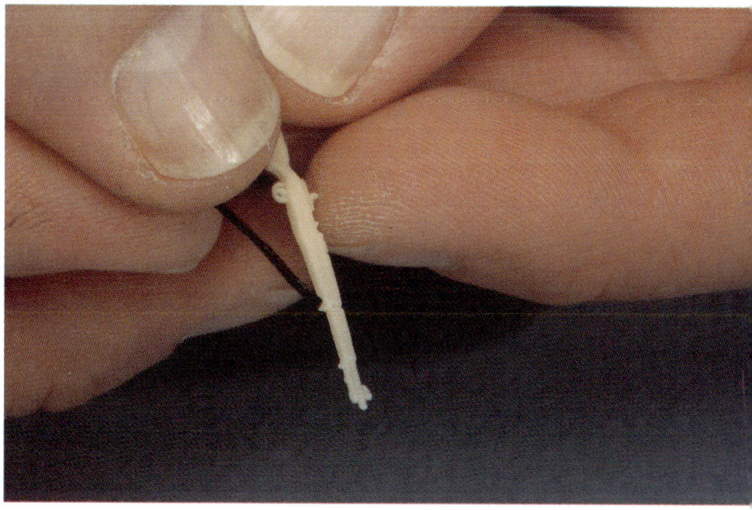

Attach the completed sling, first to one end ...

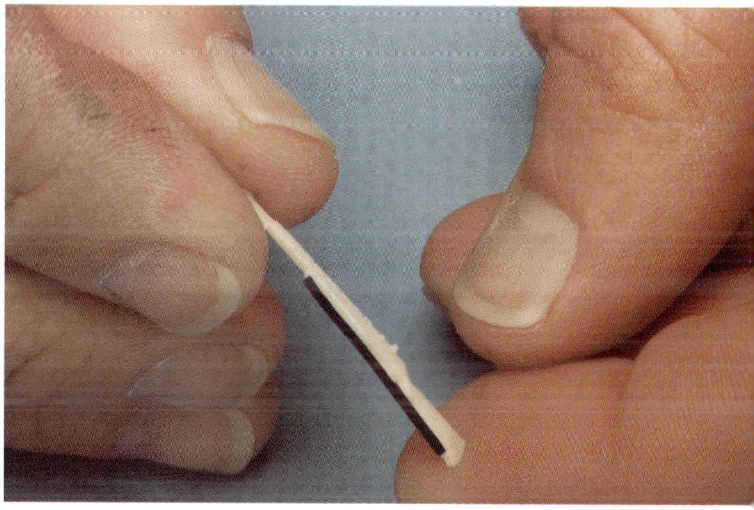

...and then to the other. The weapon is now ready to prime.

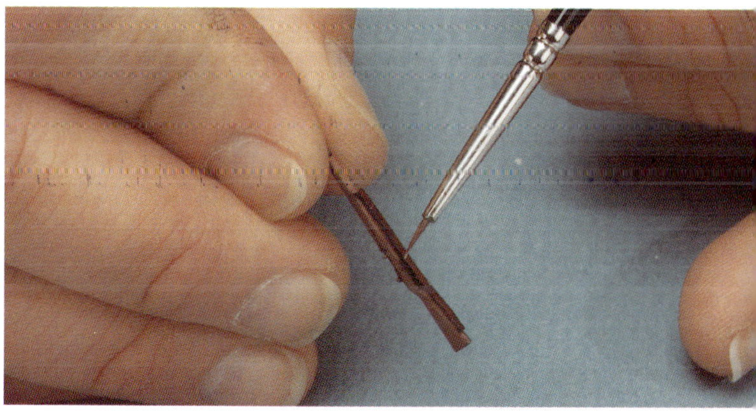

Undercoat the rifle sling with an appropriate color. For this M-1 rifle I am depicting a leather rifle sling.

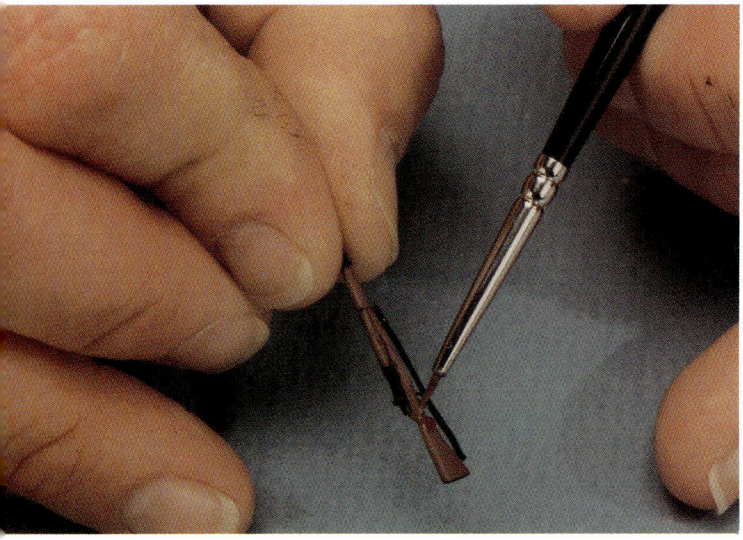

Undercoat the wooden parts of the weapon with brown hobby paint and the metal parts with black hobby paint.

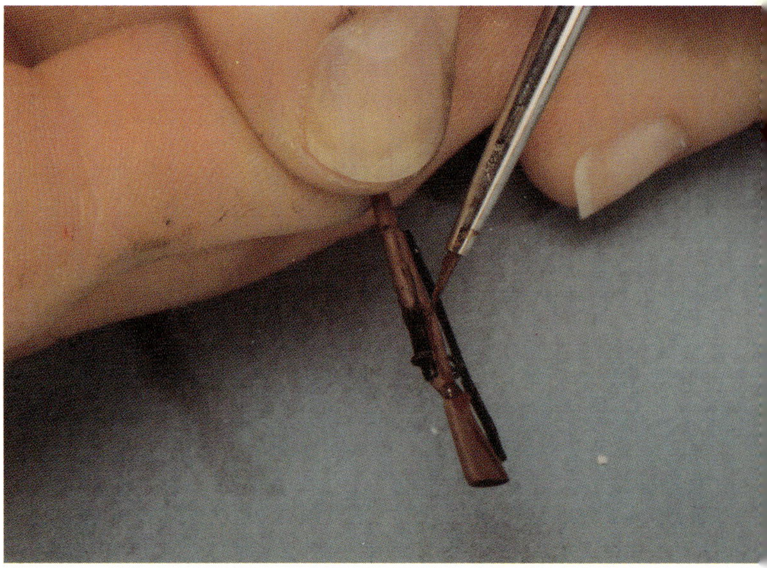

Apply the shadow color to recessed areas and outline any area where the metal parts meet wooden parts.

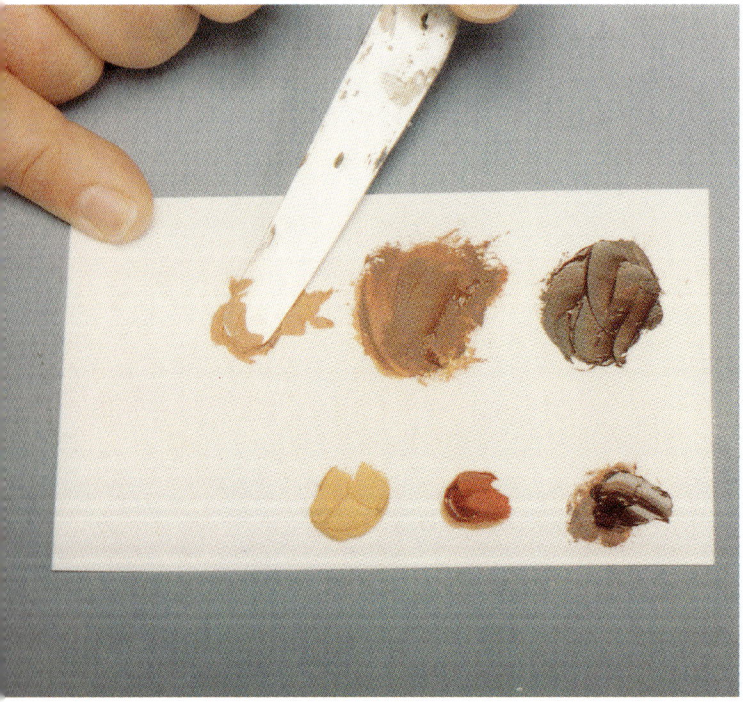

The oil colors we will use for the wood stock on the rifle are straight Burnt Sienna for the shadow color, Burnt Sienna with quite a bit of red and yellow mixed in for the middle color, with more yellow added for the highlight. The color for wooden rifle stocks will vary greatly from chocolate brown to light tan depending on the type of wood, the country of origin, and age. Many times the stocks seem to have an orange cast to them and that is why I added a considerable amount of red and yellow to the color mix.

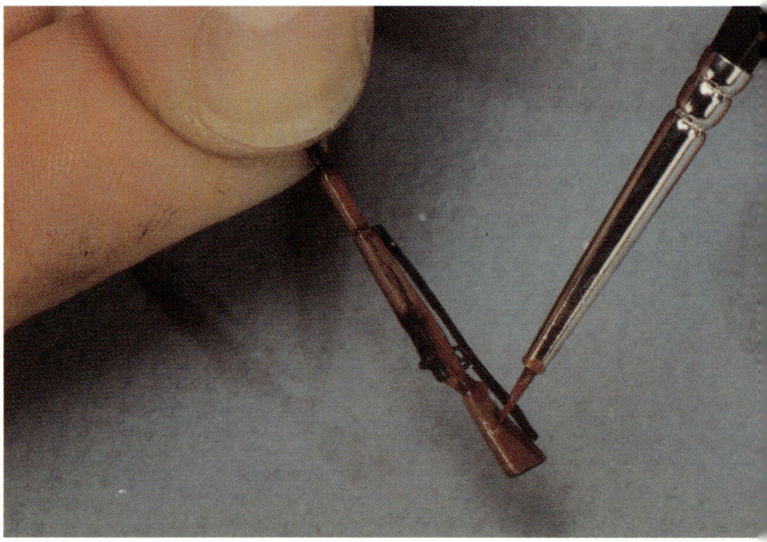

Add the middle color to the rest of the wooden areas.

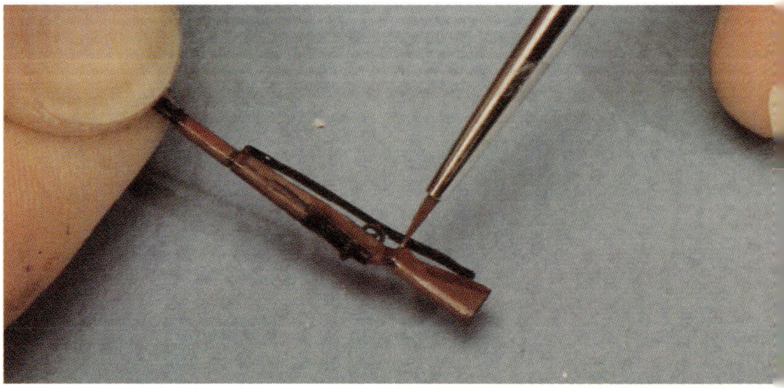

Blend the demarcation line between these two colors.

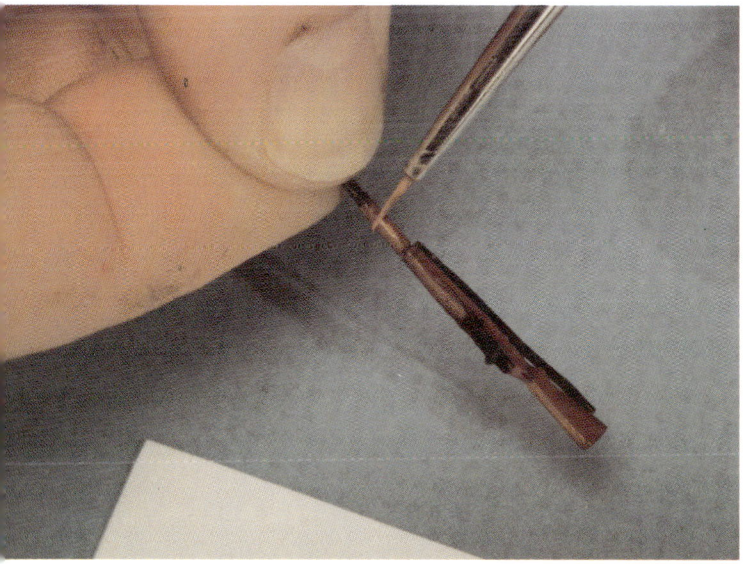

Add the highlight color to the raised areas of the rifle stock, the leading edges on the rifle butt and foregrip, for example. Carefully blend the highlights.

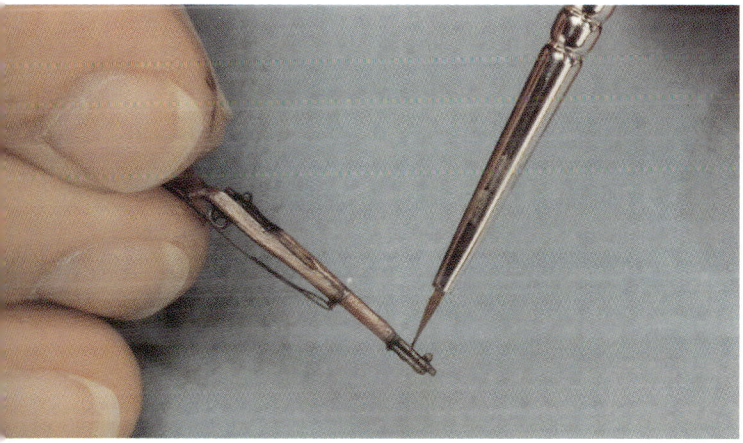

Mix black paint with a small amount of silver paint. Use the dry brush method to gently pick out the raised detail on the metal rifle parts.

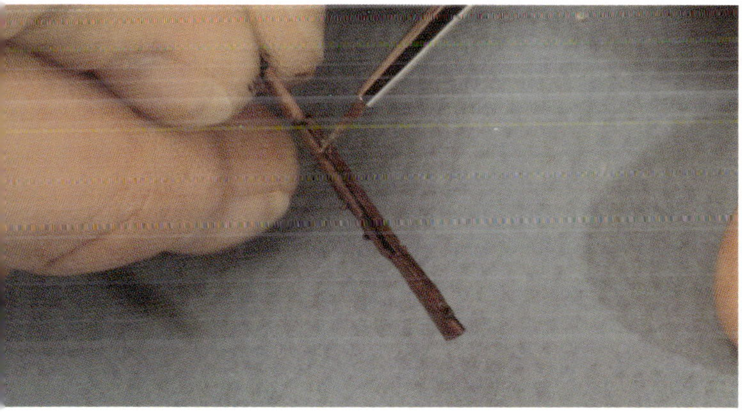

Using our three color painting method, paint the rifle sling. Place the highlight color on the outside edges of the sling and gently blend. Again, this leather color can vary greatly.

The completed rifle.

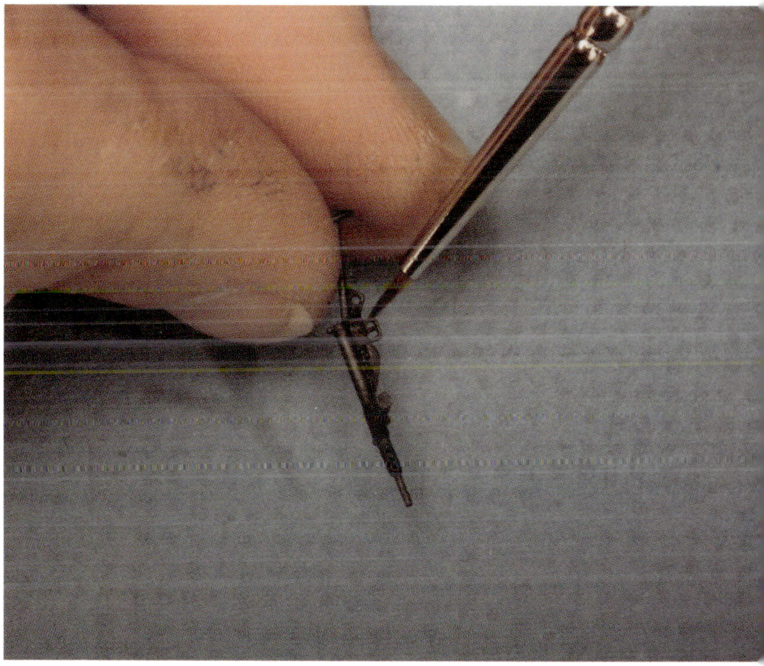

When painting weapons made entirely of metal, after undercoating in black, lightly pick out all of the details with the black and silver color mix. Use the dry brush method again.

Basic Groundwork Techniques

Attach the finished figure to its display base using five minute epoxy glue. After the glue has dried we are ready to add groundwork.

Apply real dirt that has been sifted through a piece of screen around the figure's feet.

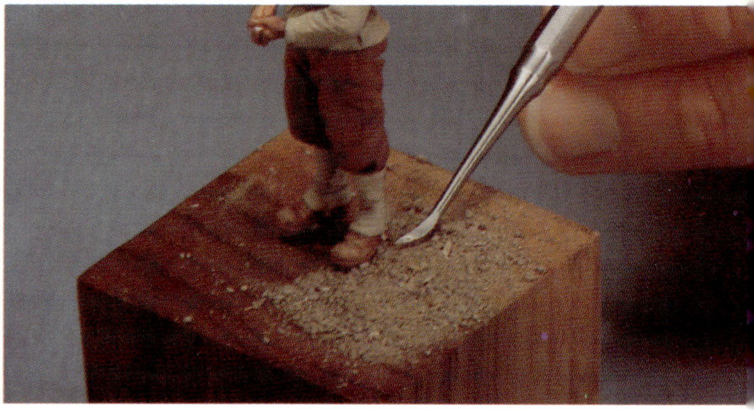

Carefully position the dirt around the feet so that it has a realistic look to it. We don't want the figure to look like he is floating off the ground, nor do we want the dirt to come up over the shoe to make it look like he is sinking into soft ground.

Using thin cyanoacrylate glue, carefully apply a drop to the surface of the groundwork. Where the groundwork turns dark, the glue has been absorbed and will stick. Where it is light, glue still needs to be applied. Continue to work your way around the base until all of the dirt is stuck in place.

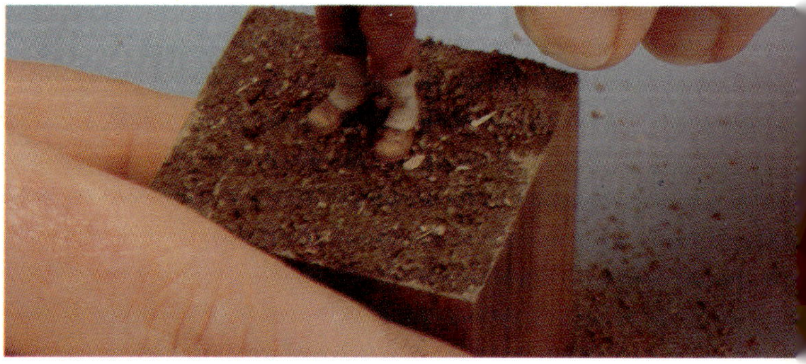

To add variety to your base, add additional dirt to show a varying topography. Once this has been positioned, glue it using the same method. If you wish to add large boulders, tree stumps, etc., glue these to the base before adding the sifted dirt.

Another way to alter the terrain is to press tank tracks into the groundwork material before applying glue. This would also work when creating footprints or any other special effects you want on your base.

The groundwork is now ready to paint. The base I created is shown beside a circular base that came with the kit. Because it has been cast in resin, it needed to be primed before painting. You do not need to prime real dirt before you begin.

Using hobby paint or hobby paint mixed with a small amount of oil paint, paint the entire surface dark brown. This will be the shadow color. If I were painting dry, arid desert-like terrain I would use a deep yellowish-tan color. Let this first color dry thoroughly.

Select a lighter shade of brown and dry brush this over the entire surface of the groundwork. I prefer to select a lighter shade of brown instead of adding white to my shadow color. This can be done using artist's oils or hobby paints.

The lighter color is now applied to the upper area of this base.

After applying your first lighter color, select or mix a color that can be used as your highlight color. Apply this in the same manner but be more selective as to the coverage area, picking out the highest points on the base.

The three colors are now applied to the upper area of the base.

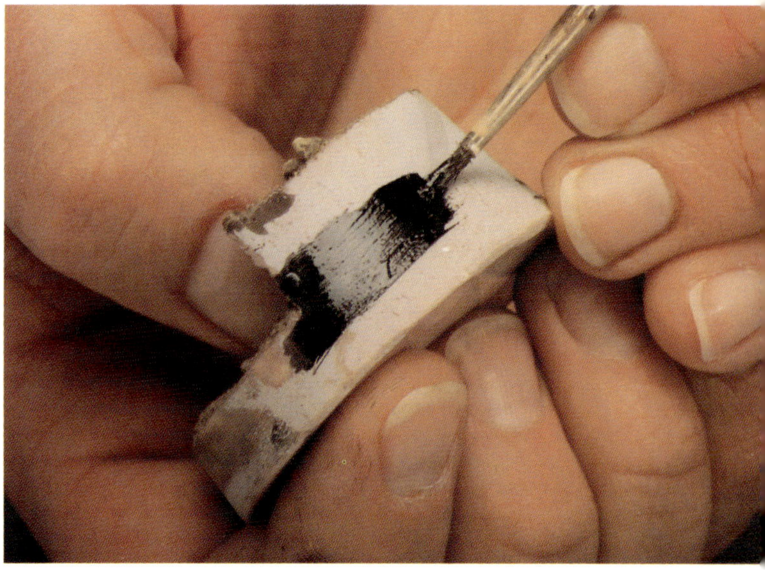

To finish this base, I painted the sides with Flat Black hobby paint.

The wooden retaining wall is also painted using the three color technique. First apply Raw Umber as the deep shadow color and then dry brush a middle color of Naples Yellow mixed with Raw Umber. As a light highlight, I mixed additional white to the middle color.

A very useful item for making grass is a product referred to as "static grass." Static grass comes in many colors ranging from green to this dark olive color.

Apply white glue in a random pattern on the figure's base.

Place a generous amount of static grass on the glue. The more you add, the better the effect.

Remove and collect any static grass that did not stick to the glue on the base. Gently blow on the grass to make it stand up.

The result. Now continue to apply grass to the rest of the base.

I recommend that you dry brush your static grass using a three color combination because many times the static grass does not look natural in its raw state. An example of a three color combination for summer grass is Sap Green as a shadow color, Sap Green and Naples Yellow for a middle color, and the middle color with additional Naples Yellow to create a highlight color.

The two German figures are examples of different amounts of static grass being used to simulate different growth patterns. The figure on the path could be standing in a well manicured park, while the mechanic is in an open field situation.

I like using a product called "Micro Balloons" when creating snow. Apply white glue to your painted display base just like we did for static grass and then place a generous amount of Micro Balloons onto the glue. Make sure your figure is completely dry or the powdery Micro Balloons will adhere to the paint.

The Micro Balloons are in place, creating the effect of partially melted snow.

Additional colors you might need are those for tropical uniforms. Usually these were tan or beige in color. A good starting point for many of these would be to mix Burnt Umber, Yellow Ochre and White together for a middle color, add additional Burnt Umber for a shadow color, and add White and a small amount of additional Yellow Ochre to create the highlight.

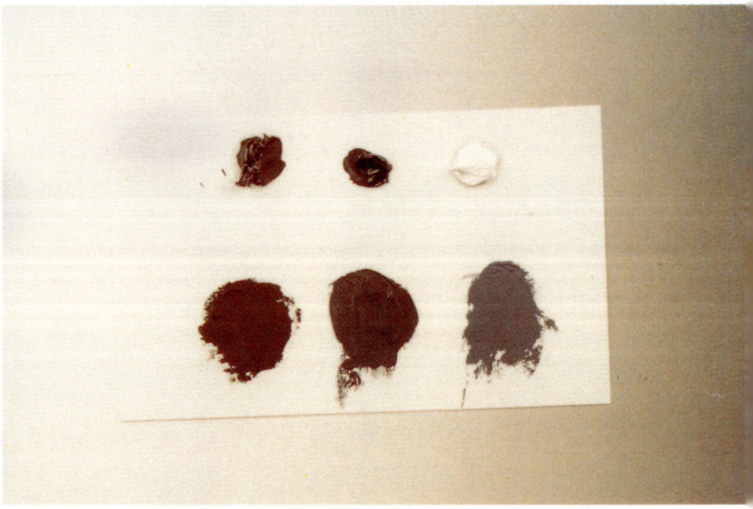

For Navy Blue uniforms mix Indigo with a small amount of Black for your middle color, add additional Black for the shadow color, and a very small amount of White to the middle color to create the highlight color. Remember to keep this highlight color very dark or you will wind up with light blue.

The Gallery